WAHHABISM:
A Critical Essay

HAMID ALGAR

WAHHABISM:
A Critical Essay

IPI

Oneonta, New York

Published and distributed by
Islamic Publications International
P.O Box 705, Oneonta, NY 13820. USA
Telephone: 800-568-9814   Fax: 800-466-8111
Email: Islampub@Islampub.com

First Edition 2002
        Algar, Hamid
            Wahhabism: A Critical Essay/
            by Hamid Algar—1 st. ed.
            p. cm.
            Includes bibliographical references and index.
            LCCN: 2001097497
            ISBN: 1-889999-13-X (paperback)
            ISBN: 1-889999-31-8 (hardback)

            1. Wahhabism—History.

            2. Wahhabism—Doctrines.   I. Title

        BP195.W2A44 2001   297.8'14
                                QBI01-201414

Director of Publications: Moin Shaikh
Cover Design: Habibur Rahman (Bounce Media) bounce@tm.net.my
Indexer: Katherine Jensen
Book Composition & Layout: David Van Ness

CONTENTS

WAHHABISM:
A Critical Essay

1

What follows is a modest survey of the history, the doctrines, and the contemporary significance of Wahhabism. Persons sympathetic to the teachings we call here "Wahhabism" might, of course, object to this designation, for it is a title given to the movement by those standing outside of it, often with pejorative intent. Wahhabis themselves prefer the titles *al-Muwahhidun* or *Ahl al-Tauhid*, "the asserters of the divine unity." But precisely this self-awarded title springs from a desire to lay exclusive claim to the principle of *tauhid* that is the foundation of Islam itself; it implies a dismissal of all other Muslims as tainted by *shirk*. There is no reason to acquiesce in this assumption of a monopoly, and because the movement in question was ultimately the work of one man, Muhammad b. ʿAbd al-Wahhab, it is reasonable as well as conventional to speak of "Wahhabism" and "Wahhabis."

Two other preliminary remarks. First, in the extremely lengthy and rich history of Islamic thought, Wahhabism does not occupy a particularly important place. Intellectually marginal, the Wahhabi movement had the good fortune to emerge in the Arabian Peninsula (albeit in Najd, a relatively remote part of the peninsula) and thus in the proximity of the Haramayn, a major geographical focus of the Muslim world; and its Saudi patrons had the good fortune, in the twentieth century, to acquire massive oil wealth, a portion of which has been used in attempts to propagate Wahhabism in the Muslim world and beyond. In the absence of these two factors, Wahhabism might well have passed into history as a marginal and short-lived sectarian movement. Those same two factors, reinforced by a partial congruity with other contemporary tendencies in the Islamic world, have endowed Wahhabism with a degree of longevity.

Second, Wahhabism is an entirely specific phenomenon, calling for recognition as a separate school of thought or even as a sect of its own. Sometimes the Wahhabis are characterized, particularly by non-Muslim observers searching for a brief description, as "extreme" or as "conservative" Sunnis, with adjectives such as "stern" or "austere" added for good measure. It has, however, been observed by knowledgeable Sunnis since the earliest times that the Wahhabis do not count as part of the Ahl al-Sunna wa al-Jama'a, for almost all the practices, traditions and beliefs denounced by Muhammad b. 'Abd al-Wahhab have been historically integral to Sunni Islam, enshrined in a vast body of literature and accepted by the great majority of Muslims. Precisely for that reason, many of the *'ulama* contemporary with the first emergence of Wahhabism denounced its followers as standing outside the pale of Ahl al-Sunna wa al-Jama'a. That Wahhabis are now counted as Sunni is one indication that the term "Sunni" has come to acquire an extraordinarily loose meaning, not extending much beyond recognition of the legitimacy of the first four caliphs (regarded by Sunnis as the Khulafa al-Rashidun ["the Rightly Guided Caliphs"]); in fact, it signifies little more than "non-Shi'i." Our characterization of Wahhabis as non-Sunni is therefore above all a historical clarification; it has in itself no polemical purpose, if only because for the present writer Sunnism is but one representation and interpretation of Islam.

Another general notion concerning Wahhabism fixed in the minds of many Muslims is that it stood

3

at the origin of a series of reform movements which in some cases are still active in the Muslim world. Thus it is imagined that a direct line of descent led from the Wahhabis in Arabia first to Jamal al-Din al-Afghani, Muhammad 'Abduh, and Rashid Rida, and from them to the Muslim Brotherhood (*al-Ikhwan al-Muslimun*)—in short, to the conglomeration of persons and movements known as the Salafiyya. There are, indeed, points held in common by Wahhabis and Salafis, as will be discussed later in this essay, and it was not entirely by accident that from the 1960's onwards many activists of the Ikhwan chose Saudi Arabia as their place of refuge from persecution by 'Abd al-Nasir. There is, however, no genetic connection between Wahhabism and movements that subsequently arose in the Muslim world. The relative prevalence of Wahhabi modes of thought now observable in various Muslim countries is a more recent phenomenon, due to a variety of contingencies unconnected with the first appearance of that sect. A related error is to think of Wahhabism as having been from the time of its origin a reform movement that found a widespread and sympathetic echo in the Muslim world, or that it conformed to a general pattern of "renewal" (*tajdid*) then underway in the Middle East, in South Asia, in

Africa and elsewhere. All those movements were largely different in their nature from Wahhabism, which must be regarded within the specific context of its own time as an exception, an aberration, or at best an anomaly.

11

Muhammad b. 'Abd al-Wahhab was born in 1115/1703 in the small town of al-'Uyayna in Najd in the eastern part of what is today called the Kingdom of Saudi Arabia. Najd had not been notable in Islamic tradition for scholarship or movements of spiritual renewal; its topographical barrenness seems always to have been reflected in its intellectual history. There are, indeed, indications in *hadith* that as a recipient of divine blessing Najd compares unfavorably with such regions as Syria and Yemen, and that it is there that "disturbances and disorder and the generation of Satan" (*al-zalazil wa 'l-fitan wa qarn al-shaytan*) will arise. Correlating apocalyptic *hadith* with observable historical phenomena is a hazardous task, best left unattempted, and this particular *hadith*, if indeed authentic, may ultimately be seen to have a sense entirely unconnected with Wahhabism.[1] However, its occurrence in the *hadith* literature does convey a sense of foreboding with respect to this part of the Arabian peninsula and suggest that any movement originating there should be viewed with great caution.

Muhammad b. 'Abd al-Wahhab's father and first teacher was the qadi of al-'Uyayna, who exercized the office in accordance with the Hanbali *madhhab* that was traditionally prevalent in the area. 'Uthman b. 'Abdullah b. Bishr, author of a standard Saudi chronicle, writes concerning the early years of Muhammad b. 'Abd al-Wahhab that "God Almighty expanded his breast for him, enabling him to understand those contradictory matters that lead men astray from His path."[2] Early anti-Wahhabi polemicists express matters quite differently: both his father and his brother, Sulayman, they report, detected signs of extreme doctrinal deviance in him at a quite early age.[3] Certain only is that Sulayman did indeed later come out against him and write the first extended refutation of Wahhabism; his father

---

[1] It may, in fact, have already found its fulfilment in the welcome accorded by the Najdis to the false prophet Musaylama al-Kadhdhab soon after the death of the Prophet.

[2] 'Uthman b. 'Abdullah b. Bishr, *'Unwan al-Majd fi Tarikh Najd*, Riyad, n.d., p. 6.

[3] See below, p. 78.

6

appears at least initially to have been more indulgent. It was as a result of the son's activities that the father was dismissed from his post and was obliged, in 1139/1726, to leave al-'Uyayna for the nearby town of Huraymila. Muhammad b. 'Abd al-Wahhab himself stayed on for a while in al-'Uyayna attempting to rectify the allegedly polytheistic tendencies of its citizens before reaching the conclusion that "words alone are of no avail" (*la yughni 'l-qaul*).[4] He therefore joined his father in Huraymila before leaving for the Hijaz, initially to perform the Hajj.

He next spent four years in Medina, which, it might usefully be pointed out, was then still an important center of Islamic knowledge and intellectual exchange, attracting scholars and students from many different parts of the Muslim world. Among those with whom he is recorded to have studied there are Shaykh 'Abdullah b. Ibrahim, a Najdi like himself, and Muhammad Hayat al-Sindi, an Indian *hadith* scholar. Particular significance is sometimes attached to the latter affiliation, for al-Sindi also numbered among his many students the celebrated Indian Sufi and *faqih*, Shah Waliullah Dihlawi. This has been taken as evidence for some degree of affinity or compatibility between Wahhabism and the

---

[4] *'Unwan al-Majd*, p. 7.

various movements of renewal in the Subcontinent that sprang from the legacy of Shah Waliullah.[5] This by no means follows, for even the most cursory comparison of Wahhabism with the infinitely richer and more profound (although frequently eccentric) teachings of Shah Waliullah immediately reveals a very great difference. Further, the mere fact that a pupil has studied with a given teacher does not necessarily mean that he has absorbed all the views of his teacher, nor that the teacher is to be held responsible for whatever notions are subsequently elaborated by the student; in other words, neither Wahhabism nor its essential constituents can be retrospectively imposed on Muhammad Hayat al-Sindi.

More significantly, Muhammad b. 'Abd al-Wahhab is said to have devoted much of his Medinan sojourn to studying the works of Ibn Taymiyya (d.728/1328), indeed a notable figure in the intellectual history of Islam, although one whose influence was probably greater posthumously than in his own lifetime. He had in common with Muhammad b.

---

[5] John Voll, "Muhammad Hayat al-Sindi and Muhammad ibn 'Abd al-Wahhab: an Analysis of an Intellectual Group in Eighteenth-Century Medina," *Bulletin of the School of Oriental and African Studies*, XXXVIII:1 (1975), pp. 32–38.

'Abd al-Wahhab a delight in polemics: his targets included Christianity; Shi'ism; many practices and doctrines of the Sufis; and the Mu'tazila, surely a questionable use of his energy, given the fact that the Mu'tazila had effectively ceased to exist. Because of the interest shown by Muhammad b. 'Abd al-Wahhab in the works of Ibn Taymiyya, it is regularly claimed that Wahhabism represents a delayed surfacing of his legacy. This claim is difficult to sustain, although less disconnected from reality than the attempt to link the founder of Wahhabism with Shah Waliullah. It is not without reason that Donald P. Little once wrote an article entitled, "Did Ibn Taymiyya have a screw loose?"[6] However, whatever one makes of the positions assumed by Ibn Taymiyya, there is no doubt that he was a far more rigorous and careful thinker and an infinitely more prolific scholar than was Muhammad b. 'Abd al-Wahhab.[7] Further, a key difference between the two men is that Ibn Taymiyya, although opposed to certain aspects of Sufism in his time which he regarded

---

[6] *Studia Islamica*, XLI: 1975, pp. 93–111.

[7] The voluminous works of Ibn Taymiyya are generally unread today by both his ardent partisans and his detractors. Ironically, an exactly parallel fate has befallen Ibn 'Arabi, Ibn Taymiyya's chief nemesis among the Sufis.

as erroneous or degenerate, did not reject it *in toto*; he was himself an initiate of the Qadiri *tariqa*.[8] By contrast, Muhammad b. ʿAbd al-Wahhab was more broadly opposed to *tasawwuf*, root and branch, not simply to certain of its manifestations. Wahhabism is essentially a movement without pedigree; it came out of nowhere in the sense not only of emerging from the wastelands of Najd, but also its lack of substantial precedent in Islamic history.

From the point of view of Wahhabism itself, it might, of course, be argued that precisely this lack of historical precedent is a virtue, the whole purpose of Wahhabism being to dismantle the complex and intricate structures of law, theology and mysticism, not to mention religious practice, that had grown up since the completion of the Qurʾanic revelation, and to find a way back directly to the twin sources of Islam, to the Qurʾan and the Sunna. At first glance, these aims might appear to be laudable, and they are no doubt shared by many Muslims who would not regard themselves as Wahhabi. Indeed, there is no binding value in what has been elaborated in history; there is binding value only in the Qurʾan and the Sunna. However, to imagine

---

[8] George Makdisi, "Ibn Taymiya: a Sufi of the Qadiriya Order," *American Journal of Arabic Studies*. I (1974), pp. 118–129.

that the meanings and applications of Qur'an and Sunna are accessible, in any substantial and usable fashion, by disregarding the virtual entirety of post-revelatory Islamic tradition, is unrealistic. It is equally illusory to suppose that either individual or society is a blank space on which Qur'an and Sunna can be authentically imprinted without admixture from either historical or contemporary circumstance. Precisely the process and mode of the Qur'anic revelation imply continuous interaction with the changing reality of human societies, a reality that necessarily includes a historical dimension.

To resume the biographical sketch. From Medina, Muhammad b. 'Abd al-Wahhab returned to Huraymila and not long thereafter, for reasons that are not immediately apparent, traveled to Basra, settling in a village by the name of al-Majmu'a. There, in the words of the Saudi historian, 'Uthman b. 'Abdullah b. Bishr, "he denounced certain things pertaining to *shirk* (*al-shirkiyat*) and innovations (*al-bida'*)."[9] It was there too that he probably had his first direct contact with Shi'i Islam. Al-Ahsa, to this day a predominantly Shi'i region despite decades of Wahhabi-Saudi persecution, borders on Najd, to its

---

[9] *'Unwan al-Majd*, p. 8. The term *al-shirkiyat* is probably the sole contribution made by Wahhabism to the technical vocabulary of Islam.

very great misfortune, but there is no indication that Muhammad b. 'Abd al-Wahhab had much substantial awareness of Shi'ism before his stay in al-Majmu'a. Now Shi'i Islam attracted his attention as allegedly rife with *al-shirkiyat*. He had, however, no success in persuading either Sunnis or Shi'is of their dire shortcomings, and he left. According to the account of 'Uthman b. 'Abdullah b. Bishr, he intended to make for Damascus (perhaps because of the presence there of Hanbali scholars), but somehow lost the money he needed for the journey, and instead returned to Huraymila by way of al-Ahsa. This was, says the Saudi historian, because "God Who knows the hidden and the apparent wished to make His cause triumph and elevate His word by uniting the people of Najd under a single leader."[10]

Another, anonymous and probably legendary, account suggests that from Basra Muhammad b. 'Abd al-Wahhab travelled to Baghdad, where he married a wealthy bride and settled down for five years. Then he is said to have proceeded by way of Kurdistan to Iran, where he visited Hamadan, Qum and Isfahan in order to study philosophy.[11] If indeed he undertook such a journey despite his antipathy

---

[10] *'Unwan al-Majd*, p. 8.

for Shi'ism, the motives that inspired him to do so are a mystery. There is no mention of Muhammad b. 'Abd al-Wahhab in the Persian sources of the period, which may mean—always supposing that he indeed visited Iran—that his attempts at propagating his notions of rectitude were disregarded there as insignificant or that he contradicted himself by making provisional use of the Shi'i practice of *taqiya* (prudential dissimulation). It is more likely, for chronological reasons alone, that he returned more or less directly from Basra to Huraymila.

There he joined his father and continued to inveigh against "ignorance, *shirk*, and innovation" with such inexhaustible zeal that his father tired of him and "words were exchanged between them" (*waqa'a baynahu wa bayna abihi kalam*), as 'Uthman b. 'Abdullah b. Bishr delicately phrases it.[12] He also found time to compile the little book called *Kitab al-Tauhid*. Despite the promise of expounding the most fundamental of all Islamic doctrines contained in the title, this booklet consists exclusively of uncommented *hadith*, arranged in sixty-seven chapters. The

---

[11] Neşet Çağatay, "Vehhabilik," *Islam Ansiklopedisi*, XIII, p. 263; anonymous, *Lam' al-Shihab fi Tarikh Muhammad b. 'Abd al-Wahhab*, ed. Ahmad Abu Hakima, Beirut, 1967.

[12] *'Unwan al-Majd*, p. 8.

late Ismail Raji al-Faruqi, in his day one of the principal promoters of Wahhabism in North America,
had it almost right when, in the introduction to his
translation to *Kitab al-Tauhid*, he described the book
as having "the appearance of a student's notes." It
would have been closer to the mark to say that this
and many other writings of Muhammad b. 'Abd al-
Wahhab *were* the notes of a student. In a flight of
fancy that would have done honor to a medieval
court panegyrist, al-Faruqi attempted to account for
the general modesty of his hero's literary output by
asserting that "he applied himself [to rectifying the
alleged misunderstanding of *tauhid* by virtually all
Muslims] with a mental vigor too great for his pen."
[13] Vigor Muhammad b. 'Abd al-Wahhab was certainly about to demonstrate, but whether it was of
the mental variety is open to question.

A brief digression on what might charitably be
termed the scholarly output of Muhammad b. 'Abd
al-Wahhab will be in order at this point. All of his
works are extremely slight, in terms of both content
and bulk. In order to justify his encomium for
Muhammad b. 'Abd al-Wahhab, al-Faruqi appended
to his translation of each chapter of the *Kitab*

---

[13] Shaykh Muhammad ibn Abd al-Wahhab, *Kitab al-Tawhid*, trans.
Isma'il al-Faruqi, reprint, Delhi, 1988, p. xv.

al-Tauhid a list of "further issues" he drew up himself, implying that the author had originally discussed some of the "issues" arising from *hadith* in the book; he had not. Similarly, an edition of Muhammad b. 'Abd al-Wahhab's *Kashf al-Shubuhat* published in Riyad in 1388/1968 has a note on the title page, "made detailed by (*qama bi tafsilihi*) 'Ali al-Hamad al-Salihi." Another book ascribed to Muhammad b. 'Abd al-Wahhab, *Masa'il al-Jahiliyya* (Madina: al-Jami'a al-Islamiya, 1395/1975), bears the notation, "expanded by (*tawassa'a fiha*) al-Sayyid Mahmud Shukri al-Alusi." In neither of the latter two cases is there any indication of where the contribution of Muhammad b. 'Abd al-Wahhab ends and where that of the elaborator begins. It seems that the custodians of Wahhabism, embarrassed by the slightness of Muhammad b. 'Abd al-Wahhab's opus, have come to regard the expansion of its girth as a necessity.

It is true that some fairly thick volumes have been published in Saudi Arabia as the collected works of Muhammad b. 'Abd al-Wahhab (*Mu'allafat al-Shaykh al-Imam Muhammad b. 'Abd al-Wahhab*, Riyad: Jami'at al-Imam Muhammad b. Sa'ud), but they are mostly a little more than collections of notes and arrangements of *hadith* according to certain subjects. The present writer has in his collection volumes one, two and four of this set; it is unclear how many volumes the complete series comprises. Volumes one and two consist entirely of *hadith* relating to regulations for ablution, prayer, and *zakat*; they contain no elucidation or commentary from Muhammad b. 'Abd al-Wahhab, and the identification of the sources of *hadith* contained in the footnotes is entirely the work of the three editors of the series.[14] Volume four opens with a brief treatise entitled *Kitab Fada'il al-Qur'an*, again a collection of uncommented *hadith* arranged in eighteen chapters. It continues with a work promisingly entitled *Tafsir Ayat al-Qur'an al-Karim*, which turns out to be little more than a series of paraphrases of some Qur'anic verses and notes on elementary grammatical points occurring in others; the only interest it exhibits lies in the occasional polemical barbs its author launches against those he calls "the leaders of *shirk*" (*a'immat al-shirk*). The volume concludes with the precis made by Muhammad b. 'Abd al-Wahhab of Ibn Qayyim al-Jauziyya's *Zad al-Ma'ad*, hardly a demanding text that would require special treatment.

Assessing Muhammad b. 'Abd al-Wahhab's accomplishments as a scholar and author is an

---

[14] The editors are 'Abd al-'Aziz b. Zayd al-Rumi, Muhammad Baltaji, and Sayyid Hijab.

entirely legitimate criterion for estimating for his broader achievement, for the history of Islam as an intellectual and spiritual tradition consists above all of its scholars and the works that they wrote; the book is the quintessential artefact of Islamic civilization. Every major figure to inaugurate a significant movement of renewal in Islamic history has been a prolific and influential writer, two examples relatively close in time to Muhammad b. 'Abd al-Wahhab being Shaykh 'Uthman dan Fodio and Shah Waliyullah Dihlawi. He is not remotely comparable to either. One has, indeed, the impression that Muhammad b. 'Abd al-Wahhab regarded the authorial act as one more unauthorized innovation that for centuries had clouded the Muslim mind.

To return from this digression to the biography. His father's death in 1153/1740 seems to have freed him from all restraint in attempting to uproot alleged manifestations of *shirk*. Although he gathered some followers, he soon found it politic to leave Huraymila and was able to return to al-'Uyayna under conditions more favorable than those prevailing some fourteen years earlier when he had been compelled to leave the city. Now the ruler of al-'Uyayna, 'Uthman ibn Mu'ammar, extended his protection to Muhammad b. 'Abd al-Wahhab and swore loyalty to the understanding of *tauhid* he was preaching. The alliance was cemented by Muhammad b. 'Abd al-Wahhab's marriage to al-Jauhara, the aunt of 'Uthman b. Mu'ammar. Thus protected by the ruler, Muhammad b. 'Abd al-Wahhab began cutting down some objectionable trees before moving on to a more ambitious demolition project: the destruction of the tomb of Zayd b. al-Khattab, a Companion of the Prophet and brother of the second caliph, who had died in the battle of Yamama fighting Musaylama al-Kadhdhab. 'Uthman b. Mu'ammar provided Muhammad b. 'Abd al-Wahhab with an armed escort of six hundred men to protect him and his small band of followers while they flailed away at the structure. It was, however, his personal lapidation of an adultress who had allegedly confessed her guilt, freely and repeatedly, that truly put Muhammad b. 'Abd al-Wahhab on the map. "Thereafter," writes 'Uthman b. 'Abdullah b. Bishr, "his cause flourished, his power increased, and true *tauhid* was everywhere disseminated, together with the enjoining of virtue and the prohibition of vice."[15]

It was precisely then that 'Uthman b. Mu'ammar yielded to pressure from a powerful tribal chieftain of the region and expelled Muhammad b. 'Abd al-

---

[15] *'Unwan al-Majd*, p. 10.

Wahhab from al-'Uyayna. The apparent setback was in fact greatly beneficial, for he moved on to al-Dir'iyya and concluded a new alliance, with Muhammad b. Sa'ud, ruler of the city, sealing it with another marriage. This alliance proved permanent, giving rise to a political entity that could for many years be interchangeably designated as Saudi or Wahhabi. In the twentieth century, it is true, the Saudi state came to acquire a second *raison d'être* as a privileged instrument of foreign—first British and then American—interests in the Middle East. In its origin, however, it was simply the political and the military arm of the Wahhabi sect. The weakening of the linkage between the religious establishment and the Saudi family now visibly underway is in its essence the inevitable outcome of a clash between these two inherited loyalties, the Wahhabi and the Anglo-American. It remains to be seen what will occur once these Siamese twins, Wahhabism and the Saudi family, are disconnected from each other and which will survive.

The now disintegrating alliance began happily enough. Muhammad b. Sa'ud pledged his aid to Muhammad b. 'Abd al-Wahhab in waging *jihad* against all who deviated from his understanding of *tauhid*. He had but one reservation: that Muhammad

b. ʿAbd al-Wahhab would prevent him from levying his customary annual tax on the people of al-Dirʿiyya. Muhammad b. ʿAbd al-Wahhab assured him that the forthcoming *jihad* would yield booty far in excess of that tax.[16] The stage was thus set for a campaign of killing and plunder all across Arabia.

In 1159/1746, the Wahhabi-Saudi state made a formal proclamation of *jihad* against all who did not share their understanding of *tauhid*, for they counted as non-believers, guilty of *shirk* and apostasy. It is significant that whenever the term "Muslims" occurs in ʿUthman b. ʿAbdullah b. Bishr's chronicle, *ʿUnwan al-Majd fi Tarikh Najd*, it refers exclusively to the Wahhabis. But the Wahhabi dismissal of all Muslims other than themselves as non-believers is of more than historical significance. Discreetly concealed over the years because of a variety of factors—above all the desire of the Saudi regime to portray itself as a protector of Muslim interests, despite abundant evidence to the contrary—this attitude of monopolistic rejection continues to inform the attitudes to Muslims held by contemporary Wahhabis and those under their influence, even when not fully articulated.[17]

---

[16] *ʿUnwan al-Majd*, p. 12.

[17] See below, p. 54.

One of the earliest historians of the Wahhabi movement, the Ottoman admiral Eyüb Sabri Pasha, drew an interesting parallel in his *Tarih-i Vehhabiyan* between Wahhabism and the movement of the Qaramita, an offshoot of the Isma'ili movement that captured Mecca in 317/930.[18] This comparison was inspired by what befell the Haramayn during the Wahhabi occupation from 1806 to 1812. Other Ottoman officials made what was perhaps a more instructive comparison, with the Kharijites.[19] At a much earlier point in Islamic history, the Kharijites had, like the Wahhabis, regarded Muslims who did not share their precise doctrines as apostates against whom war was permissible, if not obligatory, and had accordingly unleashed a campaign of banditry against them. As the Wahhabis spread out across the Arabian peninsula in the middle of the eighteenth century, their conduct and the rationale they invoked were by no means dissimilar. It is, then, in the Kharijite movement that some historical antecedent for the Wahhabis can perhaps be discovered after all, with respect not to the details of doctrine but to their mode of interaction with others.

---

[18] Eyüb Sabri Pasha, *Tarih-i Vehhabiyan*, Istanbul, 1296/1879, pp. 3–17.

[19] Neşet Çağatay, "Vehhabilik," *Islam Ansiklopedisi*, XIII, p. 267.

Contempt for non-Wahhabi Muslims has also dovetailed nicely on more than one occasion with the necessity of giving allegiance to non-Muslim powers during the twentieth century. It is noteworthy, for example, that 'Abd al-'Aziz b. Sa'ud, who ruled from 1902 to 1953, once told St. John ("Abdullah") Philby, his go-between with the British Foreign Office, that he preferred Christians to non-Wahhabi Muslims. Christians, he explained, act according to their religion, whereas the Muslims who do not follow the Wahhabi understanding of *tauhid* are guilty of *shirk*. In short, better a Christian than a non-Wahhabi Muslim.[20] It is by no means fanciful to interpret the dealings of the Saudi family with their foreign patrons as being in part the translation of such attitudes into policy.

In the fifteen years that followed the Wahhabi declaration of *jihad* large areas of Arabia were conquered. First the Saudis conquered most of Najd; then the tribes of central Arabia were subdued; and 'Asir and parts of Yemen came into their possession. Muhammad b. Sa'ud died in 1180/1766 and was succeeded by 'Abd al-'Aziz, who applied himself with still greater energy than his predecessor to the

---

[20] Elizabeth Monroe, *Philby of Arabia*, London, 1973, pp. 69–70.

expansion of the Saudi realm and the coercive propagation of Wahhabism. In 1187/1773, he conquered Riyad, and some seventeen years later began a more significant expansion of his realm by setting his sights on the Hijaz. In 1146/1733, before he had acquired Saudi patronage and support, Muhammad b. 'Abd al-Wahhab had sent a thirty-man delegation to the Sharif of Mecca, Mas'ud b. Sa'id, to obtain permission for himself and his followers to make the hajj. The Sharif discerned that part of his purpose would be to disseminate his teachings among the assembled pilgrims, and he therefore organized a debate between the visiting Wahhabis and the *'ulama* of Mecca and Medina. Muhammad b. 'Abd al-Wahhab's representatives failed to carry the day, and the *qadi* of Mecca pronounced them to be unbelievers, in view of the well-known principle, based on *hadith*, that whoever without good reason denounces a fellow Muslim as an unbeliever himself enters that category. Muhammad b. 'Abd al-Wahhab died in 1206/1791, soon after 'Abd al-'Aziz's clashes with the rulers of the Hijaz had begun, but this in no way diminished the Saudi lust for conquest and slaughter. Within less than a decade, the Wahhabi creed was to be imposed on the Haramayn—albeit temporarily—by force of arms.

The conquest of the Hijaz and the atrocities that accompanied it were preceded in 1217/1802 by a Saudi raid on the city of Karbala in southern Iraq, the place of martyrdom and burial of Imam Husayn. According to some accounts, the raid took place precisely on Muharram 10, the day on which Shi'is gather to commemorate his martyrdom. If such was the timing of the assault, it must have been deliberately chosen to inflict maximum insult and pain on the Shi'is. The matter-of-fact account of the atrocity given by the Saudi chronicler 'Uthman b. 'Abdullah b. Bishr, however, places it some three months earlier:

> In the year 1216, Sa'ud [son of 'Abd al-'Aziz] set out with his divinely supported army and cavalry that he had recruited from both the citydwellers and nomads of Najd, from the south, from the Hijaz, Tihama and elsewhere. He made for Karbala and began hostilities against the people of the city of al-Husayn. This was in the month of Dhu'l-Qa'da. The Muslims [i.e., the Wahhabis] scaled the walls, entered the city by force, and killed the majority of its people in the markets and in their homes. Then they destroyed the dome placed over the grave of al-Husayn by those who believe in such things. They took whatever they found inside the dome and its surroundings. They took the grille surrounding the tomb which was encrusted with emeralds, rubies, and

other jewels. They took everything they found in the town: different types of property, weapons, clothing, carpets, gold, silver, precious copies of the Qur'an, as well as much else—more than can be enumerated. They stayed in Karbala for no more than a morning, leaving around midday with all the property they had gathered and having killed about two thousand people. Then Sa'ud departed by way of al-Ma' al-Abyad. He had the booty assembled in front of him. He deducted one fifth for himself and then distributed the rest among the Muslims [i.e., the Wahhabis], giving a single share to each footsoldier and a double share to each horseman. Then he returned home.[21]

All in a day's work, it would seem.

The Wahhabis' first conquest in the Hijaz was the city of Ta'if, which they overran in Dhu'l-Qa'da 1217/February 1803 after a lengthy siege punctuated by various intrigues and fruitless negotiations. Here, too, they enacted a massacre, burnt books other than Qur'an and *hadith* which they found, and destroyed as many of the tombs of the Sahaba in the city as they could find. The Saudi chronicler describes the episode as follows:

'Uthman [a defector from the forces of Ghalib, the Sharif of Mecca] entered the city, together with the groups accompanying him. God enabled them to take it by force but without fighting [*sic*], and they

---

[21] *'Unwan al-Majd*, pp. 121–122.

killed some two hundred of its people, in the market-places and in their homes. They took much property, valuable items such as coins, weapons, cloth, and jewelry, beyond all measure and computation … 'Uthman sent it all to 'Abd al-'Aziz, who appointed him governor of Ta'if and the rest of the Hijaz.[22]

Some two months later, 'Abd al-'Aziz entered Mecca and compelled the *'ulama* of the city to give him *bay'a*. But this first Wahhabi occupation of Mecca was short-lived for Sharif Ghalib was able to retake the city two and a half months later.

Not long after, 'Abd al-'Aziz was assassinated in al-Dir'iyya by a certain 'Uthman, variously described as a Kurdish dervish from Mosul who had pretended to be an ardent convert to Wahhabism and as a Shi'i—possibly Afghan—from Karbala seeking vengeance for the massacre that had been enacted in that city.[23] 'Abd al-'Aziz was promptly succeeded by his son Sa'ud, the butcher of Karbala, and the campaign of conquest continued with barely a pause. In Muharram 1220/April 1805, the Wahhabi-Saudi army captured Medina and in Dhu'l-Qa'da 1220/January 1806 took possession of

---

22 *'Unwan al-Majd fi Tarikh Najd*, p. 123.

23 *'Unwan al-Majd fi Tarikh Najd*, pp. 125–126. For his allegedly Afghan identity, see 'Abbas al-'Azzawi, *Tarikh al-'Iraq bayna Ihtilalayn*, Baghdad, 1956, VI, p. 160.

Mecca for the second time. This occupation of the Haramayn was to last until the end of 1227/1812, a period of six and a half years in which Wahhabi doctrine was imposed on the people of Mecca and Medina and the Wahhabis engaged in their signature activity of dome demolition. In Mecca, the domes over the houses reputed to have been the birthplaces of the Prophet, Khadijat al-Kubra, Imam 'Ali, and Abu Bakr al-Siddiq, were destroyed, and the tombs and mausolea in the historic cemetery of al-Ma'la were levelled to the ground. In Medina, the treasury of the Prophet's Mosque was plundered but attempts to demolish the dome surmounting the grave of the Prophet were abandoned when several of the zealots entrusted with the task fell providentially to their deaths. However, all structures and gravestones in the cemetery known as Jannat al-Baqi' adjoining the Prophet's Mosque were destroyed; buried there were wives and Companions of the Prophet, several Imams of the Ahl al-Bayt, and a host of lesser luminaries from the spiritual and intellectual history of Islam. Earlier, when free of Wahhabi coercion, the *'ulama* of the Haramayn had unhesitatingly rejected the doctrines of Wahhabism; now they were compelled to submit. Among the measures imposed on them and the general population of the two cities were the compulsory performance of all five prayers in congregation; obligatory indoctrination of both scholars and common folk in Wahhabi teachings; the destruction of books deemed supportive of *shirk*—including, for example, al-Jazuli's *Dala'il al-Khayrat* and al-Yafi'i's *Raud al-Rayahin;* and a wide range of prohibitions including certain details of the prayer as specified by the Hanafi and Maliki *madhhab*s, the use of a *tasbih*, the commemoration of *Milad al-Nabi*, especially through the recitation of poetry, the traditional recitation of a number of *hadith* before the Friday sermon, the possession or smoking of tobacco, and (temporarily) the drinking of coffee. Further, the pilgrimage caravans coming from Syria and Egypt, deemed pestilential bearers of *shirk*, were denied access to the Haramayn.

The Wahhabi occupation of the Haramayn forced the Ottomans to act decisively. Their prestige as the guardians of Sunni Islam and heirs to the caliphate was dependent on at least a nominal control of the Haramayn, their actual exercise of authority being frequently contested by the Sharifs of Mecca. Some Arab historians of a nationalist bent, at least those of an earlier generation, were tempted to regard the Wahhabi movement as a proto-nationalist uprising, aimed at "freeing the Arabs from Ottoman imperial rule." More recently, the Saudi government has alleged that the first Wahhabi conquest of the Arabian peninsula aroused "the jealous attention of the Ottoman Empire" and inspired a wish "to put an end to the newly emerging nation."[24] Such characterizations are entirely anachronistic: the Wahhabi ideology had nothing to do with nationalism, and it is questionable whether a Saudi nation exists even now. It can in any event be argued that both the first emergence of the Wahhabi-Saudi state in the late eighteenth and early nineteenth century and its consolidation and expansion in the twentieth century occurred in a context of European encroachment on the Arab lands and served therefore as a factor of enfeebling division. As the historian Shaykh Ahmad b. Zayni Dahlan points out, the Ottomans were confronted at one and the same time with two "disturbances" (*fitna*s): the Napoleonic invasion of Egypt and the Wahhabi conquest of Arabia; it is, indeed, possible that the Saudis were in correspondence with the French. Nor were the French the only adversaries the Ottomans were forced to confront at this time;

---

[24] "King Fahd of Saudi Arabia," advertising supplement to *The Economist*, November 17–23, 2001.

recurrent hostilities against both Russia and Austria were also underway.

In view of these multiple preoccupations, after a series of campaigns against the Wahhabis launched by the governor of Basra had ended in failure, the Ottomans delegated the task of liberating the Haramayn to the governor of Egypt, Muhammad 'Ali Pasha. In 1226/1811 he landed at the port of the Yanbu' on the Red Sea coast, and by the end of the following year he was able to liberate Medina and three months later, Mecca. The Saudis fled back to Najd, pursued by the forces of Muhammad 'Ali Pasha, who captured and sacked their capital of al-Dir'iya in 1234/1819. Two of the grandsons of Muhammad b. 'Abd al-Wahhab were executed, and 'Abdullah b. Sa'ud was dispatched to Istanbul. There he, too, was put to death, in accordance with a *fatwa* given by Mustafa Asim Efendi, the Shaykh al-Islam of the day. Other Saudi-Wahhabis were distributed to various sites around the city for public execution in order to demonstrate the exemplary fate that the Ottomans reserved—even at this relatively late point in their history—for those who joined political ambition to religious deviance.

III

Let us now turn in somewhat greater detail to the distinctive teachings of Muhammad b. 'Abd al-Wahhab. They center on a definition of *tauhid* as consisting essentially of three parts: *tauhid al-rububiyya* (recogniton that Allah alone has the attribute of *rabb*, lord and creator of the worlds, He who gives life and death); *tauhid al-asma wa 'l-sifat* (simple affirmation of the divine names and attributes mentioned in the Qur'an, unaccompanied by any attempt at interpretation, and the impermissibility of applying to other than God any of the names, even, for example, *karim* ["generous"]); and *tauhid al-'ibada* (directing all worship to God alone).

This last is most significant from the point of view of Muhammad b. 'Abd al-Wahhab, both in his stark doctrinal scheme and in his contempt-laden assessment of the Muslim condition as it had allegedly been for many centuries. In rejection of all precedent and scholarly consensus, he dismisses the first component of *tauhid* as a mere verbal profession, of no value in itself and certainly not adequate for acquiring the quality of Muslim, for, he claims, even the polytheists of pre-Islamic Arabia believed in it.[25] He also shows no great interest in elaborating the second form of *tauhid*, beyond repeating the formulations of Ibn Taymiyya that verge on anthropomorphism. It is the third, according to Muhammad b. 'Abd al-Wahhab, that constitutes the sharp frontier between Islam and *kufr*, between *tauhid* and *shirk*. Part of his argument is that the principle of *tauhid al-'ibada* was revealed to the Prophet even before the devotional duties such as as prayer, *zakat*, fasting and pilgrimage that enabled it to be translated into practice and that it therefore has primacy over them. In just the same way that *tauhid al-rububiyya* does not suffice to make a person a Muslim, neither can he retain that quality by fulfilling his religious duties if he violates the principle of *tauhid al-'ibada* as defined by the Wahhabi sect.

Such violation takes place whenever an act of devotion involves, in any fashion at all, an entity other than the worshipper and God. The examples are numerous: petitionary prayer (*du'a*) in which mention is made of the Prophet or other exalted personages in the hope of gaining greater acceptability for one's supplication, by using a formulation such as

----

[25] See below, p. 73.

bi-hurmati ...; *isti'ana* and *istighatha*, seeking help in mundane or spiritual matters with a form of words that implies expectation of help from a given person, rather than from God, even if the person in question be implicitly viewed as a channel or transmitter of divine aid; *tawassul*, regarding a person, however exalted, as a means of facilitating one's approach to the divine presence; attributing life and agency to the dead by addressing them in a devotional context, even if not as the objects of one's devotion; the expectation of, or aspiration for, the *shafa'a* (intercession) of prophets, saints, martyrs, and other exalted personages; *tabarruk* (the seeking of blessings) at their tombs; *ziyara*, the visitation of those tombs as an act performed in its own right and with due intention; and the construction of domes or other elevated structures over such tombs. All of these result in a violation of *tauhid al-'ibada* and make of the offender a *mushrik*. To put it differently, *tauhid al-'ibada* can be defined only negatively, in terms of the avoidance of certain practices, not affirmatively; this places a fear of perceived deviation at the very heart of Wahhabism and helps to explain its intrinsically censorious nature. All the allegedly deviant practices just listed can, however, be vindicated with reference not only to tradition and consensus but also to *hadith*, as has been explained by those numerous scholars, Sunni and Shi'i alike, who have addressed the phenomenon of Wahhabism. Even if that were not the case, and the belief that *ziyara* or *tawassul* is valid and beneficial were to be false, there is no logical reason for condemning the belief as entailing exclusion from Islam.[26] For the error underlying the Wahhabi identification of all these various practices as *shirk* is a confusion of means with ends, a supposition that what is sought *from* God *by means of* a person, living or dead, is actually sought *from* that person, to the exclusion of the divine will, mercy and generosity.[27]

The corollary of identifying Muslims other than the Wahhabis as *mushrikin* was that warfare against them became not simply permissible but obligatory: their blood could legitimately be shed, their property was forfeit, and their women and children could be enslaved. As the events of Karbala and Ta'if in 1217/1803 made plain, the Wahhabis by no means shrank from the duties of butchery their doctrine imposed on them.

---

[26] See below, p. 82.

[27] It is interesting to note in passing that much nonsense has been written by Western scholars on what they term "tomb worship" or "the worship of saints" in the Muslim world, thus implicitly accepting the Wahhabi thesis that to visit and offer a prayer at a tomb, although not to its occupant, somehow constitutes a form of worship of the tomb.

A related feature of Wahhabi teaching is a capacious and undiscriminating concept of *bid'a*, innovation in religious matters. This concept has been defined as "an innovated matter not followed by the Companions or the Followers and not part of that which a legal proof (*dalil shar'i*) necessitates." It is commonly set off against the Sunna as its negative counterpart: upholding the Sunna involves the suppression of *bid'a*.[28] Broader and more positive understandings are, however, to be encountered. The Shafi'i scholar 'Izz al-Din b. 'Abd as-Salam was, for example, of the opinion that it is permissible to speak of a *bid'a hasana*, "a good innovation," and that legally all forms of *bid'a* fall into five groups: obligatory, recommended, permissible, discouraged, and forbidden.[29] Muhammad b. 'Abd al-Wahhab opted for an entirely negative and chronologically defined understanding of the concept: *bid'a* was whatever religious practice or concept had come into being after the third century of the Islamic era. The period of acceptable development thus embraces not only the first two generations of Muslims—the Companions and the Followers—but also the eponyms of the four Sunni

---

[28] Al-Sharif al-Jurjani, *Kitab al-Ta'rifat*, Beirut, 1403/1983, p. 43.

[29] Cited in Rahmi Yaran, "Bid'at," *Türkiye Diyanet Vakfi Islam Ansiklopedisi*, VI, p. 129.

schools of law. However, to engage in *taqlid* (consistent adherence to any one of those four schools) is deemed a *bid'a* insofar as it involves the apparent grant of authority to something other than the Qur'an and the Sunna. *Bid'a* had allegedly engulfed Muslim society in a host of other, more pernicious ways. The list includes but is not restricted to the various forms of *dhikr* and other ritual practised by the Sufi orders; popular customs associated with certain religiously significant dates, such as the two 'Ids; the regular invocation of peace and blessings on the Prophet as a devotional exercise, particularly when accomplished by the use of set formulae or texts such as al-Jazuli's *Dala'il al-Khayrat*; and any commemoration of the birthday of the Prophet, especially when accompanied by formal ceremonies and, again, the recitation of texts such as al-Barzanji's celebrated *qasida*. Muhammad b. 'Abd al-Wahhab's belief that *bid'a*—not to mention *shirk*—had deluged the Muslim community for some nine hundred years was one of the several factors that set him apart from movements of renewal contemporary with him. They held to the traditional perception that the Muslim community stood in periodic need of renewal and purification and that this need would be met, in accordance with a certain *hadith*, with the appearance of a *mujaddid* ("renewer") once every hundred years. From the point of view of Muhammad b. 'Abd al-Wahhab, it seems no such renewer had appeared since 299 Hijri, or that if he had, he had failed to check the exuberant proliferation of *bid'a*, so that Islam had been in abeyance as a practised reality for six hundred years or more. Muhammad b. 'Abd al-Wahhab thus not only denounced and fought his contemporaries; he was also at war with their ancestors.

I V

*O*nce the troops of Muhammad 'Ali Pasha departed, the Saudi-Wahhabi movement gradually regrouped in its homeland of Najd, establishing a new capital in Riyad and, about a decade later, taking control of al-Ahsa. Similarly, in 1248/1832, a military expedition against Uman persuaded the sultan of Muscat to pay tribute to Riyad. The eastward direction of this new wave of expansion was fortuitous in that it ultimately brought the Saudis into contact with the British who were not only seeking to consolidate their dominance of the Persian Gulf but also beginning to lay plans for the dismemberment of the

Ottoman State.[30] The first contact was made in 1865, and British subsidies started to flow into the coffers of the Saudi family, in ever growing quantity as World War One grew closer. The relationship fully matured during that war. In 1915, the British signed with the Saudi ruler of the day, 'Abd al-'Aziz b. Sa'ud (Ibn Sa'ud), one of those contracts with their underlings that were euphemistically known as "treaties of friendship and cooperation". Money was, of course, the principal lubricant of friendship and cooperation, and by 1917 the Saudi ruler was receiving five thousand pounds a month, not a bad sum for a junior hireling of the British Empire. However, the

---

[30] It may be as well to address here the conspiracy theory that attributes the very origin of Wahhabism itself, not simply the Kingdom of Saudi Arabia, to British devilry. The theory is enshrined in the so-called *Mudhakkirat Mister Hempher*, the purported memoirs of a British agent in the Middle East in the early eighteenth century subtitled *al-Jasus al-Britani fi 'l-Bilad al-Islamiyya*. The alleged memoirs exist, remarkably enough, only in Arabic, into which language they have supposedly been translated by an otherwise unidentified Dr. J. Kh. The only English version in existence, published by a group of anti-Wahhabi enthusiasts in Istanbul, has obviously been translated from the Arabic, and clumsily at that. "Mr. Hempher", it seems, so thoroughly assimilated his role as undercover agent that he used the Hijri calendar in preference to the Christian. Among other clues to the inauthenticity of the work are references to the desirability of encouraging nationalism as a means of sundering Islamic unity—this, at a time when nationalism had barely appeared even in Europe—the advisability of promoting birth control in order to block demographic growth in the Muslim world, and the need to displace Arabic by promoting "local languages such as

British also graciously saw fit to confer a knighthood on the champion of Wahhabism.[31] (In later years these formalities continued to be observed; in 1935, 'Abd al-'Aziz b. Sa'ud was made a Knight of the Order of the Bath. Likewise, when visiting Queen Elizabeth in 1986, King Fahd, "Custodian of the Two Holy Mosques," was photographed with the cruciform insignia of a British knightly order hanging round his neck).[32] British demands of the Wahhabi-Saudi statelet were initially fairly modest:

Sanskrit." Given the frequency of positive references to Shi'ism in the book, it seems likely that the author was Shi'i. He would have done better to leave the task of refuting Wahhabism to scholars such as Shaykh Ja'far Kashif al-Ghita', from whose treatise an extract is included at the end of this essay. The copy of "Hempher's memoirs" in the possession of the present writer, acquired in Tehran, is dated at the end 1.2.1973, the significance of which is unclear; no place of publication is indicated.

[31] In their zeal to control the Middle East after the conclusion of World War One, the British were quite busy minting medals and distributing knighthoods. Among those to benefit from their largesse at this time was 'Abd al-Baha', son of Baha'ullah, the inventor of Baha'ism. Although one of his followers lauded him as "the innermost mystery of God" (*sirrullah*; see E.G. Browne, *A Literary History of Persia* (Cambridge, 1924, IV, p. 207) , 'Abd al-Baha' graciously consented in 1920 to accept a title of somewhat less elevated nature— Knight of the British Empire (Alessandro Bausani, "'Abd-al-Baha'," *Encyclopaedia Iranica*, I, p. 103). The rain of imperial favor thus fell with ecumenical impartiality on Wahhabi and Baha'i alike.

[32] For a full color photograph of this historic encounter, see Fouad al-Farsy, *Custodian of the Two Holy Mosques King Fahd bin Abdul Aziz*, Guernsey, Channel Islands, 2001, p. 214. It is unknown whether the curious infatuation with Margaret Thatcher to which King Fahd

to have its armies—thoughtfully provided with British weapons and instructors—attack the Banu Rashid, the principal allies of the Ottomans in north-eastern Arabia, and to deny the Ottomans themselves any foothold on the southern shore of the Persian Gulf. These duties were faithfully performed.

Matters were, however, a little complicated; the British had not yet given Ibn Sa'ud a licence to conquer the whole Arabian peninsula. In accordance with the cunning that proverbially characterized their machinations, they had more than one collaborator in Arabia at the time. For they were also in contact with the ruler of Mecca, Sharif Husayn, progenitor of the Hashimite dynasty that has continued to produce loyal servants of foreign interests down to the present (such persons are commonly designated as "moderate Arab rulers" in the parlance of the Western media), impelling him by means of financial and other inducements to rise up against the Ottomans in the name of a unified Arab nation of which he was to be king. Significant is that the British imposed on Sharif Husayn as a condition for their support that he should recognize the privileged position of the Saudis in Najd and the rest of eastern Arabia.

---

confessed in later years contributed to further strengthening the foundations of Anglo-Saudi amity.

The aftermath of the First World War and its repercussions in the Arabian peninsula are well known. Two rival British officials—each remarkably unpalatable in his own right, even by the undemanding standards of the British ruling class in its heyday—pressed the competing claims of their respective Arabian proteges: T.E. Lawrence jousted on behalf of the Hashimites and St. John ("Abdullah") Philby championed the Saudis.[33] Sharif Husayn proved guilty of the childish error of believing that Britain's wartime promises of a unified Arab state to be established under his auspices were to be taken seriously, and he became a nuisance. Moreover, unlike the Saudis, he lacked a disciplined fighting force, one capable of taking control of the whole peninsula and providing the stability deemed essential for British imperial interests; this, Ibn Sa'ud possessed, in the form of the notorious Ikhwan, the shocktroops and enforcers of Wahhabism. The Hashimites were therefore dropped and the green light was given to

---

[33] The fortunes of Lawrence and Philby came to mirror the destinies of their respective proteges to a considerable extent. Sharif Husayn lost the Pan-Arab kingdom he had been promised, and Lawrence lost his head, crushed in a freak motorcycle accident. Ibn Sa'ud conquered most of the peninsula, and Philby was rewarded with the lucrative Ford dealership for the Wahhabi kingdom, not to mention a succession of adolescent brides placed hospitably at his disposal.

Ibn Saʿud to conquer the entirety of the Arabian peninsula. Far from being a spontaneous or autonomous development, the extension of Saudi control across the peninsula should therefore be placed in the context of the general reconfiguration of the Middle East that was then underway, largely under the charitable auspices of the British, ever generous with lands that were not theirs. It formed part of the same pattern as the division of the Arab lands of the Fertile Crescent into artificial units; the implantation of Zionism in Palestine under the protection of the British mandate; the establishment of the "secularist" Turkish Republic; and the rise of the Pahlavi dynasty in Iran.

Nor was the establishment of the Kingdom of Saudi Arabia a peaceful affair. The second Wahhabi-Saudi conquest of the peninsula came at a cost of some 400,000 killed and wounded. In cities such as Taʾif, Burayda, and al-Huda, straightforward massacres were carried out by the Ikhwan. The governors of the various provinces appointed by Ibn Saʿud are said to have carried out 40,000 public executions and 350,000 amputations in the course of subduing the peninsula. The majority Shiʿi population of al-Ahsa received special attention: Ibn Saʿud appointed his cousin, ʿAbdullah b. Musallim b. Jilawi, perhaps the foremost butcher of the family after the monarch himself, to subjugate them, which he did by executing thousands of people and decimating both the religious and tribal leadership of the Shi'i community. Mecca and Medina, conquered by the Saudis in 1925, were disfigured again with the imposition of Wahhabi tenets and practices. A renewed attempt at destroying the dome of the Prophet's Mosque failed, but numerous historic sites that had survived the first Wahhabi occupation were now demolished.[34] (It is curious that while Wahhabi doctrine is obsessively concerned with the evils of domes over tombs, the towering palaces erected by the Saudi monarchs have somehow escaped the strictures of the elders of the sect). In the name of "enjoining the good and forbidding the evil," smoking was again prohibited, men were punished for not wearing beards of sufficient length, music was outlawed, and flowerpots deemed to offend public

---

[34] For evidence that the destruction of historic sites with blessed associations from the earliest period of Islam continues down to the present as a matter of explicit Wahhabi-Saudi policy, see Elaine Sciolino, "Where the Prophet Trod, He Begs, Tread Lightly," *New York Times*, February 15, 2002. Of particular interest in this article is its citation of *fatwa* 16626, issued in 1994 by 'Abd al-'Aziz b. 'Abdullah b. Baz, which reads in part: "It is not permitted to glorify buildings and historical sites. Such action would lead to *shirk* because people might think the places have spiritual value."

decency with their bright colors were smashed.[35] It is true that some of these measures fell into abeyance when the necessity of compromise with Muslim sentiment concerning the management of the Haramayn imposed itself. It is, however, indisputable that the millennial role of the Haramayn as centers of Islamic scholarship and intellectual exchange, populated by teachers and students from places as far apart as Central Asia, the Malay-Indonesian world, Subsaharan Africa, and India, was now definitively at an end. The dead hand of Wahhabism has left nothing in place. With the exception of small, semi-clandestine teaching circles, all that is now to be found in Mecca and Medina are institutes for the propagation of Wahhabism, grotesquely mislabelled as universities.

The subsequent history of the Saudi family, its acquisition of oil wealth, and the switch from Britain to America as principal foreign patron, are beyond the scope of this essay. It will, however, be appropriate to note the ongoing attempts of the Saudi regime to propagate Wahhabism outside Arabia.

We have remarked above that Wahhabism had little positive echo outside the Arabian peninsula

---

[35] On all these developments, see Said K. Aburish, *The Rise, Corruption and Coming Fall of the House of Saud*, London, 1994, pp. 20–27.

when it first appeared on the scene. Some confusion on this point has been created by Western writers who have affixed the Wahhabi label to a number of Islamic movements that bore little if any resemblance to the Wahhabi sect, a notable case in point being the Ahl al-Hadith group in India. The Tsarist, Soviet and post-Soviet authorities have similarly labelled as Wahhabi virtually all movements of Islamic resistance to Russian rule in the North Caucasus and Central Asia. (This attribution to Wahhabism of universal expansion was perhaps the earliest example of the Western tendency to connect any and all Islamic movements to a single and invariably maleficent source). The only nineteenth century movement the origins of which can confidently be traced to Wahhabism was the Padri uprising in the Minangkabau highlands of Sumatra, led by a certain Haji Miskin who had been in Mecca during the shortlived Wahhabi occupation of 1803.[36]

Coercion and further military expansion as a means of such propagation were excluded as early as 1929 once Ibn Sa'ud's British masters had dissuaded the Ikhwan from encroaching on Iraq by means of

---

[36] See Christine Dobbin, *Islamic Revivalism in a Changing Peasant Economy: Central Sumatra, 1784–1847*, London and Malmö, 1983, pp. 128–149.

aerial bombardment, their preferred method of keeping order in the Middle East. As for peaceful propagation, the earliest publicists for the resurgent Saudi regime were, curiously enough, two Arab Christians: Amin Rayhani and George Antonius. However, a Muslim champion from outside the Arabian peninsula was not long in emerging. This was Rashid Rida (d. 1935), who as early as 1909 had been accused in his native Syria of Wahhabism.[37] After a visit to the newly conquered Hijaz, he published a work praising the Saudi ruler as the savior of the Haramayn and a practitioner of authentic Islamic rule and, two years later, an anthology of Wahhabi treatises.[38] We may recall that the aftermath of World War One saw both the abolition of the Ottoman Caliphate and the failure of Sharif Husayn to gain either a pan-Arab kingdom or acceptance by Muslims as candidate for a revived caliphate. It is, then, perhaps not surprising that persons of Salafi tendency such as Rashid Rida, casting around in desperation for a hero, should have begun to view Ibn Sa'ud with favor and to express sympathy for Wahhabism.

---

[37] On Rashid Rida's early tendencies to Wahhabism, see David Dean Commins, *Islamic Reform: Politics and Social Change in Late Ottoman Syria*, Oxford, 1990, pp. 129–131.

[38] Rashid Rida, *al-Wahhabiyyun wa 'l-Hijaz*, Cairo, 1344/1926; Rashid Rida, ed., *Majmu'at al-Tauhid al-Najdiyya*, Cairo, 1346/1928.

The Salafiyya had, after all, certain elements in common with Wahhabism, above all disdain for all developments subsequent to *al-Salaf al-Salih* ("The Righteous Ancestors," generally taken to be the first two generations of Islam), the rejection of Sufism, and the abandonment of consistent adherence to one of the four Sunni *madhhab*s. Some four decades after the Saudi conquest of the Hijaz, the Salafi movement—especially in Egypt—took a more radical turn and began describing the state of contemporary Muslim society to be neo-Jahiliyya.[39] It may be permissible to discern in this development a delayed echo of the Wahhabi dismissal of all Muslims as *mushrikin*. Two important and interrelated features have usually served, however, to distinguish the Salafis from the Wahhabis: a reliance on attempts at persuasion rather than coercion in order to rally other Muslims to their cause; and an informed awareness of the political and socio-economic crises confronting the Muslim world.

In any event, it was not until the 1960's that a closer association of Salafis with Wahhabism came about, the result not only of the broad propagation

---

[39] This is exemplified above all by Sayyid Qutb (d. 1966) in his various works, most famously in *Social Justice in Islam*, trans. John B. Hardie (New York, 2000), and by his brother, Muhammad Qutb, in his *Jahiliyyat al-Qarn al-'Ishrin* (Cairo, 1964).

of Wahhabism fuelled by petrodollars, but also of the political circumstances in the Arab world. What has aptly been called the Arab Cold War was then underway: a struggle between the camps led respectively by Egypt and its associates and Saudi Arabia and its friends. Threatened by the popularity of Jamal 'Abd al-Nasir, the Saudi regime elaborated a diverse strategy for ensuring its survival. On the military front, it fought a proxy war with Egypt in Yemen, and on the political front it engaged in much publicized exercises in "Islamic solidarity" with such implausible champions of Islam as President Bourguiba of Tunisia and the Shah of Iran.[40] And on the ideological front, it established in 1962—not coincidentally, the same year as the republican uprising in neighboring Yemen—a body called the Muslim World League (*Rabitat al-'Alam al-Islami*).

It was in the bosom of this organization, intended to eclipse all other supranational Islamic organizations, that a closer association between leading Salafis

---

[40] It is significant that when a credibly Islamic order did emerge in Iran as the result of revolution, Saudi Arabia was among the most energetic and determined opponents of the nascent Islamic Republic; "Islamic solidarity" across the waters of the Persian Gulf was quickly forgotten. Indeed, in 1981, the Saudis gave $10 million to a colonel in the Iranian Air Force to stage a coup which was to include the bombing of the residence of Imam Khomeini in north Tehran; the coup was promptly discovered and foiled.

and Wahhabis came into being. Its constituent council, which met for the first time in December 1962, was headed by the then chief *mufti* of Saudi Arabia, Muhammad b. Ibrahim Al al-Shaykh, a lineal descendant of Muhammad b. 'Abd al-Wahhab, and the presidency remains to this day vested in the Saudi chief *mufti*. Included among its eight other members were important representatives of the Salafi tendency: Sa'id Ramadan, son-in-law of Hasan al-Banna, founder of the Muslim Brotherhood of Egypt, and a claimant to his mantle; Maulana Abu 'l-A'la Maududi (d. 1979), leader of the Jama'at-i Islami of Pakistan; and Maulana Abu 'l-Hasan Nadvi (d. 2000) of India. In accordance with statute, the head of the league's secretariat has always been a Saudi citizen, the first to occupy the post being Muhammad Surur al-Sabban (d.1972). Members of the Egyptian (and later Syrian) Muslim Brotherhood could hardly be faulted for thus aligning themselves with Saudi Arabia, given the persecution to which they were subjected in their homelands, and it may also be argued that these Salafis were able somewhat to soften the harshness of traditional Wahhabism, at least at the institutional level. Others had no such excuse, and there was, in any event, a political price to be paid: support, explicit or implicit, for the policies of the Saudi government, for article four of the Muslim World League's covenant committed it to work for the establishment of "Islamic solidarity" as articulated by the Saudi regime.[41]

The Muslim World League has done its best to live up to its title by establishing branch offices around the globe; these are concentrated in Europe, South and South East Asia, and most particularly Africa. Part of the function of these offices is, as it is delicately phrased on the website of the League, to "repel inimical trends and dogmas." This generally means the propagation of Wahhabism at the expense of local Islamic traditions, a task in which returning graduates of the so-called Islamic University of Medina also enthusiastically participate. Deeply rooted Sufi traditions are condemned as *bid'a*, a destructive and divisive activity especially in African countries where the practice of Islam is often coterminous with adherence to a Sufi *tariqa*. The celebration of Mawlid al-Nabi also comes under attack, with similar results.[42]

Some Muslim student organizations have also functioned at times as Saudi-supported channels for the propagation of Wahhabism abroad, especially in

---

[41] For a comprehensive account of the Muslim World League, see Reinhard Schulze, *Islamischer Internationalismus im 20. Jahrhundert: Untersuchungen zur Geschichte der islamischen Weltliga*, Leiden, 1990.

[42] Remarks based in part on a visit to Nairobi, Mombasa, Malindi and Lamu Island in 1985.

the United States. The Muslim Student Association of North America and Canada was established in 1963, one year after the Muslim World League with which it had close links. Particularly in the 1960's and 1970's, no criticism of Saudi Arabia would be tolerated at the annual conventions of the MSA; King Faisal was regarded as a fearless champion of Islam. Its numerous local chapters would make available at every Friday prayer large stacks of the League's publications, in both English and Arabic, and generally did their best to prevent the dissemination of "inimical trends and dogmas." The intellectual mentor of the MSA leadership was for many years the late Ismail al-Faruqi, mentioned above for his heroic efforts to elevate the intellectual status of Muhammad b. 'Abd al-Wahhab. Although the MSA progressively diversified its connections with Arab states, official approval of Wahhabism remained strong; as late as 1980 its publishing arm saw fit to produce the translation ("expansion"?) by al-Faruqi of three treatises by Muhammad b. 'Abd al-Wahhab under the heading *Sources of Islamic Thought*. It might appear at first sight puzzling that students pursuing a higher education should be attracted to a Wahhabi reading of Islam. In a sense, however, the attraction was natural: attuned to a rationalistic worldview fostered by their studies of engineering and the natural sciences, they found in Wahhabism a "rationalized Islam," one already stripped of the niceties and ambiguities of juristic reasoning, the complexities of theology, and the subtleties of Sufism, all of these having been decried as "accretions." It might be argued that in this particular sense al-Faruqi's apparently extravagant assertion that "al-Dir'iyya became the greatest capital of Islamic modernism without undergoing any modernist influence" was actually true.[43] In 1980, the original MSA branched into a student organization, still bearing the same title, and a new body called the Islamic Society of North America. ISNA is currently the largest Muslim organization in the United States and as such reflects—although not in equal measure—the wide array of inclinations and preferences prevalent in the community. Similarly, the hundreds of Muslim student groups now active in the United States reflect a diverse range of opinions and resist any uniform characterization.

Collaboration between the original MSA and analogous organizations elsewhere in the world resulted in the foundation in 1966 of the International Islamic Federation of Student Organizations, a body described as having "close relations

---

[43] Introduction to translation of *Kitab al-Tawhid*, p. xiv.

with the Muslim World League." The IIFSO over-
laps with the World Assembly of Muslim Youth, the
secretary general of the former being an ex-officio
member of the board of trustees of the latter.
Established in 1972, the WAMY is headquartered,
by remarkable coincidence, in Riyad.[44] Noteworthy,
too, is the somewhat elastic understanding of
"youth" cultivated by some of its perennially leading members in its first decade.

A widely circulated organ of Wahhabi teaching is
the magazine *al-Jumu'ah*, an English-language peri-
odical established in 1991, prepared by "teams" in
the United States, London, and Saudi Arabia, and
billing itself as "your guide to an Islamic life." It
devotes itself to "correction of creed" (*tashih al-
'aqida*, i.e, the refutation of non-Wahhabi interpretations of Islam) and the publication of *fatwa*s,
mostly prohibitive in nature, touching on the details
of everyday life. It is, however, far from a gloomy
publication: printed on glossy paper, it even includes
photographs of living persons, curiously truncated,
however, in observation of the Wahhabi ban on even
the two-dimensional representation of living beings.
Also worth noticing is an English translation of the

---

[44] Sayyid Muhammad Syeed, "International Islamic Federation of
Student Organizations," *Oxford Encyclopaedia of the Modern Islamic
World*, Oxford, 1995, II, pp. 207–209.

Qur'an by Muhammad Taqi al-Din al-Hilali and Muhammad Muhsin, printed in Riyad in 1994 and bearing the imprimatur of the Saudi mufti, 'Abd al-'Aziz b. 'Abdullah b. Baz.[45] The translators state in their afterword, *inter alia*, that "we have noticed that most of the mankind, who embrace Islam, [*sic*] do not understand the reality of the meaning of the first fundamental principle of Islam, *Lâ ilâha ill Allâh, Muhammad-ur-Rasûl-Allâh* (none has the right to be worshipped but Allah, and Muhammad—peace and blessings be upon him—is the Messenger of Allâh)."[46] Lurking behind this awkward euphemism is the classical Wahhabi condemnation of the great majority of Muslims as guilty of *shirk*.

Despite all these efforts, Wahhabism has by no means universally triumphed. In many parts of the Middle East, the Sufi orders have shown a resilience and vitality that have confounded Wahhabis and Western scholars alike. Certain areas of the Muslim world are, however, particularly vulnerable to Wahhabism, especially those now emerging from decades of communist rule and war. It is undeniable

---

[45] One wonders whether the mufti's command of English was sufficient for judging the accuracy of the translation.

[46] *Interpretation of the Meanings of the Noble Qur'an in the English Language*, Riyad, 1994, p. 1011. I have retained the transliteration of the *kalima* found in the original.

that Wahhabism has made progress in the Central
Asian republics as well as the North Caucasus,
although certainly to a lesser degree than is claimed
by Moscow. The misery suffered by the Bosnian
Muslims in recent years has been accentuated by the
efforts of various outsiders, Wahhabis prominent
among them, to propagate their own understandings
of Islam at the expense of local tradition. This has had
an architectural as well as a creedal dimension. As if
the depredations carried out by Serbs and Croats during the war were not enough, Wahhabi exertions in
Bosnia have included defacement in the name of
restoration. In the Gazihusrevbegova Džamija, the
principal mosque of Sarajevo, the decorations on the
walls have been covered with whitewash, so that were
it not for the carpets on the floor, the interior of the
mosque would have all the aesthetic charm of a hospi-
tal ward. Plaques affixed to the wall next to the
entrance of this and other mosques remind the worshipper that the "restoration" he is about to behold is
due to Saudi generosity; in some cases, the plaques
have been defaced by ungrateful Bosnians. A newly
built mosque in Zenica, similarly devoid of mural
decoration, is also due to Saudi funding, as the worshipper is encouraged to remember whenever he
goes into prostration, for every segment of the rug

covering the ground is marked with the bilingual inscription, in Arabic and Bosnian, "a gift from the Kingdom of Saudi Arabia."[47] Wahhabi vandalizing of Islamic monuments in Kosova, Chechnya, and Hadramaut has also been reported.

There is reason for regarding the perverse, incompetent and now happily defunct regime of the Taliban as a manifestation of Wahhabism, although its *fiqhi* underlay was Hanafi rather than Hanbali and the movement owed its cohesion also to a generous investment by Pakistan of its military and intelligence resources. Official Saudi contacts with the Taliban began in 1995 when Maulana Fazlur Rahman, leader of the Pakistani Jami'at-i 'Ulama-yi Islam, arranged for a party of Saudi princes to go hunting in the region of Qandahar. Ideological considerations were, however, more important for the Wahhabi scholars than the pleasures of the chase in boosting the cause of the Taliban. Persuaded that they had found diligent recruits to their cause, they successfully lobbied the Saudi regime to extend a brotherly hand to the Taliban.[48] In April 1997, a

---

[47] Observations based on the present writer's visits to Bosnia in 1998 and 1999.

[48] Ahmed Rashid, *Taliban: Militant Islam, Oil and Fundamentalism in Central Asia*, New Haven and London, 2000, p. 201.

member of the Taliban leadership, the late Mulla Rabbani (not to be confused with Burhanuddin Rabbani, the pre-Taliban president of Afghanistan now back in business in Kabul courtesy of the United States Air Force) paid a visit to Riyadh at the conclusion of which he was able to remark: "King Fahd expressed happiness at the good measures taken by the Taliban and over the imposition of *shariʻa* in our country" (cited by Robert Fisk, "Saudis Turn Their Backs on the Taliban," *Independent*, September 27, 2001). The especially venomous hostility displayed by the Taliban to the Hazaras—including a massacre of some 5000 after the second Taliban conquest of Mazar-i Sharif in 1998 as well as more recent atrocities in the area of Bamiyan and the enslavement of Hazara women as concubines—is to be explained in large part by the Shiʻi identity of that people.[49] Likewise reminiscent of classical Wahhabism were measures such as the prohibition of small and harmless joys such as the flying of kites by children, the

---

[49] The following should in fairness be mentioned. In an audience with Ayatullah Sayyid ʻAli Khamenei in June 1997 at which the present writer was present, two representatives of an Afghan Shiʻa organization complained of the allegedly inadequate assistance Iran was providing them in their struggle for suvival. In his response Ayatullah Khamenei reproached the organization in question for employing in its conflict with the Taliban the same brutality of which they justifiably stood accused. He had in mind presumably the massacre of the

insistence on regulating the details of facial hair, the forced performance of prayer in congregation, and the pitiless exclusion of women from all forms of social and economic activity.[50] The demise of the Taliban regime does not necessarily mean, however, that the days of Wahhabism in Afghanistan are over: 'Abd al-Rasul Sayyaf, one of the leaders of the so-called Northern Alliance, is as much a convinced Wahhabi as any of the Taliban leadership, and was responsible for the sectarian killing of Shi'is during the days of anarchy in Kabul that preceded the rise to power of the Taliban.

The Wahhabi scholars of Saudi Arabia have nonetheless been sorely troubled by the end of the Taliban regime. In an undated declaration posted on a Wahhabi website on December 5, 2001, ten of them deplored the consequences of the entry into Kabul of the Northern Alliance—described as "consisting of Communists, Shias, and hypocrites"—as follows: "They opened up shrines of *shirk* which the Taliban had shut [the Sufi *khanaqah*s are presumably

---

Taliban garrison in Mazar-i Sharif that had occurred the previous month; this could be classified as either a sensible precaution or an act of revenge, given the mass killings of Shi'is in which the Taliban had already engaged elsewhere in Afghanistan.

[50] For a sample of Taliban decrees, see Ahmed Rashid, *Taliban*, pp. 217–219.

what is meant], shaved the beards, threw away the *hijab*, spread music and singing, along with showing movies." It remains uncertain whether the Northern Alliance will prove a lesser evil than the Taliban, but what is striking in the fulminations of these sages is their complete indifference to the real and acute sufferings of the Afghan people and their censorious concentration on issues of the type mentioned. A similar callousness can be deduced from their assessment of the attack on the World Trade Center as "divine retribution." What offenses meriting divine punishment had been committed by thousands of people going about their daily business is a mystery, unless one espouses a Qur'anically untenable belief in collective guilt. The ten eminent scholars are also of the opinion that "the fear and outbreak of diseases in its [September 11's] aftermath" is an instance of "the Ways of Allah" (*sunan Allah*). It strikes the present writer as little short of blasphemous to suggest that the death of unsuspecting postal workers from handling anthrax-laden mail is somehow a manifestation of the divine will and wisdom.[51]

---

[51] "Important Declaration from Ten Scholars after Taliban withdrawal," www.as-sahwah.com. The signatories are 'Abd ar-Rahman b. Salih al-Mahmud, Ahmad b. Salih al-Sinani, Sa'd al-Humayd, 'Abd al-'Aziz b. Muhammad Al 'Abd al-Latif, 'Abd al-'Aziz b. Nasir al-Jalil, Hamd b. Ris, Farih b. Salih al-Bihlal, Hamd b. 'Abdullah al-Humaydi, and Nasir b. Hamd al-Fahd.

As for the Arabian homeland of Wahhabism, the historical alliance between the Wahhabis and the Saudi family has been unravelling for some time. The uprising in Mecca at the beginning of November 1979, led by a certain Juhayman Muhammad 'Utaybi, represented a sudden and unexpected resurgence of the Wahhabi Ikhwan; it was put down by French paratroopers who were given special dispensation by Wahhabi scholars loyal to the Saudi regime to enter the Masjid al-Haram and kill the rebels by flooding the mosque and electrocuting them.[52] It was, however, the Gulf War of 1991 and the vast expansion in the American military presence accompanying it that led to a further estrangement between Wahhabis and the Saudi regime. Given the presence of British officers in Najd as early as World War One and the longstanding American airbase at Dhahran, it was hardly a novelty for the Saudi regime to invite for-eign forces to entrench themselves in Arabia (or, perhaps more accurately, to consent to their doing so). Nonetheless, the new bases were correctly interpreted as intended to be more obtrusive, per-

---

[52] Said K. Aburish, *The House of Saud*, p. 118; *Intifadat al-Haram*, a booklet published by Munazzamat al-Thaurat al-Islamiyya fi 'l-Jazirat al-'Arabiyya (Organization of the Islamic Revolution in the Arabian Peninsula), n.p. (Tehran?), n.d.

manent and extensive than anything that had gone before. Regarded as almost equally outrageous was the phenomenon of a number of women taking to the wheel and driving themselves around Riyad. A number of Wahhabi scholars denounced these developments, chief among them being Safar b. 'Abd al-Rahman al-Hawali and Salman b. Fahd al-'Auda, who were rewarded for their pains with prolonged imprisonment.

It is worth noting that concerns about the American presence and the cultural consequences thought liable to flow from it did not displace the long-standing Wahhabi obsession with Shi'ism. In a sermon on the topic of "What God has decreed for this [Arabian] Peninsula" (*Qadar Allah fi hadhihi 'l-Jazirah*), the same Salman b. Fahd al-'Auda stressed what he regarded as the centrality of Wahhabism to the welfare of Arabia (conceived of as the heart, not merely in a geographical sense, of the entire Muslim world) and as a corollary he called for the expulsion of all its Shi'i inhabitants, referred to by the traditional pejorative of *al-rafida*[53]. Worse,

---

[53] Cited by Mamoun Fandi, *Saudi Arabia and the Politics of Dissent*, New York, 2001, p. 101. This demand was not new. As early as 1927, the Wahhabi *'ulama* issued a *fatwa* that threatened with expulsion all the Shi'is of al-Ahsa unless they consented to the destruction of their mosques and to indoctrination in Wahhabism. The *fatwa* was never

'Abdullah b. Jibrin delivered in 1991 a *fatwa* condemning Shi'i Muslims as *"mushrikin* whose blood may be shed." Perhaps in a move to divert righteous Wahhabi wrath from itself, the Saudi regime moved the following year to imprison and execute a number of its Shi'i subjects and razed to the ground four Shi'i mosques.[54]

Al-Hawali and al-'Auda are by no means unaware of developments in the outside world, and validity is not to be denied to some at least of their theses concerning the Gulf War and the American political process. However, they have had no direct experience of the West, and have correspondingly remained virtually unknown there. Different on both counts are two other oppositional figures, each in his own way a continued adherent of Wahhabism, Muhammad al-Mis'ari and Sa'd al-Faqih.

The first is the current leader of the the Committee for the Defence of the Legitimate Rights (*Lajnat al-Difa' 'an al-Huquq al-Shar'iyya*), a body established in May, 1993 by a council of *'ulama* at

---

enforced, for political reasons. See Jacob Goldberg, "The Shi'i Minority in Saudi Arabia," Juan R. Cole and Nikki R. Keddie, eds., *Shi'ism and Social Protest* (New Haven ,1986), pp. 235–236. The continuing attractiveness for Wahhabi *'ulama* of the expulsion option inevitably calls to mind the Zionist project of "transfer," i.e., completely emptying Palestine of its indigenous population.

[54] Said K. Aburish, *The House of Saud*, pp. 110–111.

the head of which stood his father, Shaykh ʿ
al-Misaʿri.[55] Muhammad al-Misʿari, who acted as
spokesman for the council, was detained on May 15
and a propaganda campaign was launched against
the Committee, to which it responded with a clarification of its aims on May 26. The signatories
emphasized the reformist nature of their goals,
claiming that they were entirely consistent with
existing institutions, and affirmed in conclusion that
"all the members of the committee believe in the
creed of the Ahl as-Sunnah and observe the norms
of this creed as far as the attitude to rulers is concerned."[56] This assertion was meant no doubt to
convey two messages: that the members of the
Committee, despite official insinuations to the contrary, had no connection to Shiʿism but were loyal
Sunnis (read: Wahhabis), and that they intended to
respect the traditional ban on rebellion against
authority implied by that label. It was, in fact, in
Najd, the homeland of Wahhabism, that the decla-
rations and communiques of the CDLR were most

---

[55] *Arabia Monitor*, II:5 (May 1993), p. 1. The other members of the
council were Hamd al-Sulayfiyyah, ʿAbdullah b. Jibrin (author of the
genocidal *fatwa* against the Shiʿis), ʿAbdullah al-Hamid, and ʿAbdullah
al-Tuwaijiri. See Fandy, *Saudi Arabia and the Politics of Dissent*, pp.
118–119.

[56] *Arabia Monitor*, II:6 (June 1993), p. 4.

eagerly greeted. Muhammad al-Mis'ari relocated to London some time in 1994, and taking advantage of the media possibilities available there he effectively became head of the organization and began publicizing the misdeeds of the Saudi regime from exile.[57] In 1995, he went beyond the originally reformist goals of the group by publishing a work entitled *al-Adillat al-Qat'iyya 'ala 'Adam Shar'iyyat al-Daulat as-Sa'udiyya* ("Decisive Evidence for the Illegitimacy of the Saudi State"). Perhaps most remarkable in this book was his criticism of Muhammad b. 'Abd al-Wahhab himself for first entering on an alliance with the Saudi family which had, in his view, deprived the Wahhabi call of its allegedly universal purpose.[58] There is nonetheless an echo of Wahhabism in his political scheme, for the ideal Islamic state of which he conceives would bar the Shi'i citizens of Saudi Arabia from holding positions of influence.[59] The

---

[57] Ultimately unsuccessful attempts to silence al-Mis'ari or even to have him deported from Britain to Dominica in the West Indies provided an interesting illustration of the strong ties still existing between Britain and the Saudi regime. The British government of the day tried to justify its stance by pointing to massive impending arms deals with Saudi Arabia that tolerance of al-Mis'ari was allegedly endangering.

[58] *Al-Adillat al-Qat'iyya 'ala 'Adam Shar'iyyat al-Daulat as-Sa'udiyya*, p. 233.

[59] Fandy, *Saudi Arabia and the Politics of Dissent*, p. 146.

picture is, however, mixed, for more recently he has engaged in dialogue with Shi'i scholars resident in London such as Ayatullah Muhsin Araki, and given an interview to the Islamic Republic News Agency.[60]

As for Sa'd al-Faqih, he began his career as an activist with the CDLR, but broke with it (or, according to al-Mis'ari, was expelled from it) in 1996 in order to establish a new organization, the Movement for Islamic Reform (*al-Harakat al-Islamiyya li 'l-Islah*), which would preserve the original aims of the CDLR. If this statement of purpose be more than the result of organizational infighting with Muhammad al-Mis'ari, it necessarily means that Sa'd al-Faqih also grounds his movement in loyalty to Wahhabism. His organization is said, indeed, to follow Hanbali *fiqh* narrowly and to "anchor its interpretations and discourse" in the writings of Muhammad b. 'Abd al-Wahhab as well as Ibn Taymiyya and Ibn Qayyim al-Jauzyiyya; however, it prefers the rubric of Salafi to that of Wahhabi. Sa'd al-Faqih proclaims himself ready to accommodate the Shi'is but explains his refusal to make friendly overtures to representatives of the

---

[60] Fandy, *Saudi Arabia and the Politics of Dissent*, p. 173.

community in terms of the prejudices of his constituency in Arabia.[61]

It is impossible to measure the support within Saudi Arabia for the CDLR or the MIRA. But for a number of Wahhabi *'ulama* within the country, matters seem to have reached a point of no return in the aftermath of September 11, 2001, and the somewhat hesitant support given by the regime to the American assault on Afghanistan. *Fatwas* have been delivered by Shaykhs Hamud al-Shu'aybi and 'Abdullah b. Jibrin which not only justify the attack on the World Trade Center—sensitively dismissing as so much "babbling" all talk about innocent victims—but also condemn as apostates any and all Muslims collaborating with America, a category obviously including the Saudi family.[62] The two *raisons d'être* of the Saudi regime—subservience to external powers and adherence to the Wahhabi sect—are now proving increasingly incompatible. It is devoutly—in the literal sense of that word—to be hoped that if the Saudi monarchy collapses, something other than a retrograde Wahhabi regime will emerge from its ruins.

---

[61] See Fandy, *Saudi Arabia and the Politics of Dissent*, pp. 161–162, 173.

[62] *Fatwas* posted on www.as-sahwah.com , October 15, 2001.

V

It will be abundantly clear to the attentive reader by now that the present writer has little liking or sympathy for Wahhabism. He would therefore like to offer the following clarificatory remarks by way of conclusion.

First, it is a matter of common Muslim experience that Wahhabis and those under their influence have been liberal with accusations of *shirk* and *bid'a* for many years. This deplorable practice has now been inverted. Individuals with dubious credentials and motives who have appointed themselves upholders of Ahl al-Sunna wa al-Jama'a ("moderate," "mainline," and "traditional" are some of the attributes with which they seek to adorn themselves) charge with Wahhabism all who do not subscribe to their views on politics and religion. It is significant that in their eagerness to win the favor of certain circles these professional anti-Wahhabis charge with Wahhabism particularly those Muslims for whom the cause of Palestine remains a high priority. No doubt the Salafi mode of thought has many adherents, and no doubt it has points in common with Wahhabism, as suggested above. However, it is inaccurate, irresponsible, and dangerous—particularly in the climate of post-September 11 America—to conflate "Salafi" with "Wahhabi" and paint a picture of American Muslims as being in their majority Wahhabi.[63]

Second, the critical attention now being paid to Wahhabism in the West proceeds largely from two sources: outrage that those responsible for the crimes of September 11 came, for the most part, from a Wahhabi background; and annoyance that Wahhabi activists and preachers have increasingly prevented the Saudi regime from fulfilling to complete satisfaction its allotted role in American schemes for political and military domination of the Middle East. The first of these is entirely legitimate; the second, less so. The current heightened awareness of Wahhabism comes also in the context of an open-ended American war against a terrorism that insofar as it is defined at all is something ascribed only to Muslim persons, organizations, or states. This war is being waged in concert with allies such as Russia, its hands bloodied with the

---

[63] There is, indeed, some justice to the observation of Shaykh Salih Al al-Shaykh, the Saudi minister of Islamic affairs, that in the Western media praying in a mosque has become a "hardline practice. Then they equate hard-liners and terrorists, and we all become terrorists." *New York Times*, December 4, 2001.

Muslims of Chechnya; China, that has taken advantage of the opportunity to oppress with greater ferocity than before the Muslims of Eastern Turkistan [Sinkiang]; and Uzbekistan, where praying in a mosque can lead to years of imprisonment and torture. Worse still, it comes at a time of intensified genocidal rampaging in Palestine by the Zionists with the full backing of the United States.

Apart from noting with disgust the repugnant endorsement by certain Wahhabis of the atrocity commited against the innocent in New York on September 11, the author's primary intention is unconnected to the present conjuncture. What has inspired this essay, first drafted more than a year ago, is rather a concern that the Wahhabis have seriously distorted fundamental teachings of Islam; functioned for many decades as the ideological mainstay of a regime that has squandered the wealth of the Arabian peninsula; vilified Muslims, both Sunni and Shi'i, as non-Muslim and shed their blood; introduced or exacerbated division and strife wherever they have gone; destroyed a significant part of the cultural patrimony of all Muslims, first in the Hijaz and then in places such as Chechnya, Bosnia, and Kosova; and signally failed to contribute anything to either the intellectual elaboration of Islam or the advancement of its political and civilizational agenda in the present age.

APPENDICES

A
From the Writings of Muhammad b. 'Abd al-Wahhab:

It is difficult to find passages of continuous expository writing from the founder of Wahhabism which might serve to illustrate faithfully his particular mode of thought, for most of his writings consist of assemblages of *hadith*, as pointed out above. Others have been subjected to "expansion," which is the case with the work from which the following extracts are taken. There is, however, no reason to doubt that the leading ideas it contains are authentically his, apart from which the mode of expression is appropriately inelegant. Noteworthy is his contention that the *mushrikun* of Arabia whom the Prophet confronted were all effectively monotheists, save only for their belief in intermediaries. This utterly inaccurate portrayal of the Meccan polytheists helps to explain the ease with which Muhammad b. 'Abd al-Wahhab condemned as *mushrik* the Muslims of his time. Indeed, he regarded the Muslims who were his contemporaries as more reprehensible than those against whose false beliefs the

Prophet had struggled, as the second of these extracts makes plain; this accounts, perhaps, for the Wahhabi recourse to a ferocity that the Prophet was never tempted to permit himself in his battles. It is remarkable, too, that in the second extract Muhammad b. 'Abd al-Wahhab discerns sinlessness and piety in inanimate objects.

In explanation that the primary task of the Messengers was to establish *tauhid* of worship:

Know, may God have mercy upon you, that *tauhid* is worshipping God in exclusivity, this being the religion of all the messengers whom He sent to His servants. The first of them was Noah, whom God sent as messenger to his people when they exaggerated concerning the righteous, namely Wida, Wiswa' Yaghuth and Nasr. The last of the Messengers was Muhammad, peace and blessings be upon him; he it is who broke the images of those righteous people. God sent him to people who were engaged in worship, pilgrimage, the giving of charity, and making abundant remembrance of God. However, they made certain creatures intermediaries between themselves and God, saying "we seek to come close to God by means of them and we seek their intercession," [creatures] such as the angels,

Jesus, Mary, and other people from among the righteous.

So God sent Muhammad, peace and blessings be upon him, to them, in order that he might renew for them the religion of their forefather, Abraham, and inform them that approaching and believing (*al-taqarrub wa 'l-i'itiqad*) belong exclusively to God, no part of them being fit for an angel drawn near to the divine presence or a prophet sent by Him, let alone anyone else. For otherwise those *mushrikun* bore witness that God alone is the creator, without any partner; that He alone gives sustenance; that He alone gives life and death; that the heavens and all they contain, the seven layers of the earth and all they contain—all is subject to His disposal and power.

—(*Kashf al-Shubuhat*, expanded by 'Ali al-Hamad al-Salihi, Riyad, 1388/1968, pp. 13–14).

Proof that the *shirk* of the ancients was less grave than that of the people of our age:

Once you realize that what the *mushrikun* in our time call *al-i'tiqad*[64] is the *shirk* to which the Qur'an

---

[64] What is meant by *al-i'tiqad* is the belief that certain personages possess, especially posthumously, properties that make their intercession with God acceptable.

refers and on account of which the Messenger—
peace and blessings be upon him—fought against
people, know too the following: that the *shirk* of
earlier generations was slighter than that of the
people of our age, for two reasons.

The first is that the ancients did not, in times of
prosperity, assign partners to God nor did they call
on angels, sacred personages (*al-awliya'*), and idols.
As for times of hardship, they directed their petitionary prayer exclusively to God. The proof is this
saying of God: "When distress seizes you at sea,
those upon whom you call abandon you, all except
Him, and when He brings you safely to shore, you
turn away. Surely man is ungrateful" (*al-Isra'* 67).
Again, "Say: Think to yourselves—if the punishment
of God comes to you, or the Hour arrives, will you
call upon other than God? Reply if you are truthful.
No, it is on Him alone you would call; He would
relieve you of the distress occasioning your call upon
Him, if He so wished, and you would forget the partners you assigned Him" (*al-An'am*, 40–41).[65] Also
pertinent are the verses, "When distress touches

---

[65] The verses cited hardly prove Muhammad b. 'Abd al-Wahhab's
argument. On the contrary, the first establishes that the *mushrikun* did
call upon other than God when facing danger at sea, and the verses
from *Surat al-An'am* invites them to ponder on a future situation in
order to remedy their current state.

man, he calls penitently on his Lord, but when He bestows on him a favor from Himself he forgets what had earlier prompted that calling upon Him; he sets up rivals to God in order to mislead others away from His path. Say: Enjoy your unbelief for a short while; certainly you are one of the companions of Hellfire" (*al-Zumar*, 8), and "When a wave covers them like a shade, they call upon God in exclusive devotion" (*Luqman*, 32).

Let then this matter be understood as God has clarified it in His book: the *mushrikun* whom the Messenger—peace and blessings be upon him— fought called upon God and called upon others [at the same time] when they were at ease.[66] As for times of distress and hardship, they called upon God alone, the Unique and One without partner, forgetting their masters. This should suffice to make clear to you the difference between the *shirk* practised by the people of our time and the *shirk* of the ancients. But where are those who have the understanding of this question rooted in their hearts? May God come to our aid.

The second reason for the greater guilt of the people of our times is that the ancients used to call

---

[66] This sentence seems to contradict the statement contained in the opening of the second paragraph of this extract.

upon persons close to God, prophets, friends of God, or angels, or direct their petitionary prayers to trees and rocks, objects obedient to God, not rebellious against Him. As for the people of our time, they call upon the most sinful of men together with God. Of those whom they beseech for aid it is related that they commit gross sins such as adultery, theft, the abandonment of prayer, and so on. The offense of one who believes in the power of a righteous man or of an object, like wood or stone, that does not rebel against God, is less grave than that of one who has a similar belief concerning one whose sinfulness and corruption are manifest.

—(*Kashf al-Shubuhat*, pp. 31–32).

B

A near-contemporary view of early Wahhabism

Ahmad b. Zayni Dahlan, born in 1232/1816, became the Shafiʻi *mufti* of Mecca in 1288/1871 and died there in 1304/1886. He cannot therefore be regarded as an eyewitness to the events that befell the Haramayn during the first Wahhabi occupation, but he was acquainted with many of those who had lived through it. The following extract from his major historical work, a chronicle of the Islamic world after the demise of the Prophet, may therefore serve to reflect attitudes to Wahhabism that were current in the Hijaz two or three decades later.

The founder of this vile sect, Muhammad b. ʻAbd al-Wahhab, originated in the eastern part of the Arabian peninsula among the tribe of the Bani Tamim. He lived for almost a hundred years, which enabled him to spread his misguidance. He was born in the year 1111 and he perished in the year 1206, as expressed in this chronogram:

The destruction of the vile one became apparent (*badâ halâk al-khabîth*).

He began as a student of the religious sciences in al-Madina al-Munawwara, peace and blessings be upon the one dwelling there [the Prophet]. His father was a righteous scholar, as was his brother, Shaykh Sulayman. Together with his teachers, both of them began to suspect that he would give rise to error and misguidance, on account of various sayings, acts and tendencies they observed in him. They reproached him and warned people against him. God proved their suspicions to be justified when by way of unjustified innovation (*bid'a*) he propagated error and misguidance, leading the ignorant astray in opposition to all the established leaders in matters of religion (*a'immat al-din*). He went so far as to declare the believers unbelievers. He claimed that visiting the tomb of the Prophet—upon whom be peace and blessings—as well as appealing to him or other prophets and righteous persons as intermediaries (*al-tawassul*) or visiting their tombs constituted *shirk* [the assignation of partners to God]. He also denounced as *shirk* addressing the prophets, the saints, and the righteous when appealing to them, and attributing anything to other than God, even if by way of rational metaphor. Thus if someone were to say, "this medicine benefited me," or "such-and-such saint aided me when I appealed to him as an intermediary," that person would be guilty of *shirk*.

In all of this, Muhammad b. 'Abd al-Wahhab cited proofs that in no way supported his arguments. So he concocted deceptive and fair-seeming phrases by means of which he persuaded the common people to follow him, writing treatises which convinced them that most of the people of *tauhid* were in fact unbelievers. He then established contact with the rulers of the eastern part of the peninsula, especially al-Dir'iyya, and took up residence among them until he persuaded them to support him and propagate his cause. They made of that a means for strengthening their rule and expanding it over the Beduins and the desert dwellers. Those Beduin thus came to serve as a volunteer army for them, convinced that whoever does not believe in what Muhammad b. 'Abd al-Wahhab says is an unbeliever, guilty of *shirk*, whose blood may legitimately be shed and whose property plundered. The beginning of this affair was in 1143, and it began to spread in 1150.

The scholars wrote numerous treatises in refutation of Muhammad b. 'Abd al-Wahhab; included among them were his own brother, Shaykh

Sulayman, and his teachers.... But he claimed that the aim of the sect he originated was to purify *tauhid*, to free it from all trace of *shirk*, the state in which people had allegedly been for six hundred years, and to renew their religion for them.

—(*Tarikh al-Futuhat al-Islamiyya*, Cairo, 1387/1968, II, pp. 234–235).

C

A Shi'i Response to Wahhabism

In 1210/1795, some eight years before the Wahhabi
sacking of Karbala, Shaykh Ja'far Kashif al-Ghita'
(d. 1228/1813), one of the leading Shi'i scholars of
the time, addressed to 'Abd al-'Aziz b. Muhammad
b. Sa'ud an elegantly and courteously worded treatise entitled *Manhaj al-Rashad li man arada 'l-Sadad*.
Drawing exclusively on Sunni books of *hadith*, he
sought to refute the many accusations of *kufr* and
shirk that Wahhabis were levelling against the
Muslims—including *par excellence* the Shi'a. The following extract deals with the question of *istighatha*,
the seeking of help from sacred personages, and
related practices deemed *shirk* by the Wahhabis but
a well-established and firmly grounded part of both
Sunni and Shi'i devotional tradition. Important is
the author's observation that neither belief in the
permissibility of such practices nor the rejection
thereof is integral to faith in Islam.

I beseech you by the One Who bestowed on you
hearing and vision: ponder this matter carefully and

purify your soul from all desire to stand apart from others, this being incumbent upon us just as is the avoidance of adhering unquestioningly to our fathers and ancestors out of pure love.

There is no difference between the living and the dead [with respect to invoking them], for seeking help (*al-istighatha*) from a created being or seeking refuge in him on the assumption that he is an independent agent (*fa'il mukhtar*) is indeed a species of unbelief (*kufr*). Such is the case with [the invocation] of Jesus and Mary [presumably the author is alluding here to Christian beliefs or practices—translator]. But the simple belief that the dead can either hear or not hear invocations made to them is not a doctrine of religion the knowledge of which is incumbent on the Muslims. The one who holds either of these positions is either in the right and will be rewarded, or he is in the wrong and will be forgiven.

Now words that convey hope or trust placed in other than God, reliance upon other than God, seeking refuge (*al-iltija'*) in or aid from other than God, if taken in their literal sense, would not leave any Muslim on the face of the earth. For there is no one who does not seek aid against his enemies, who does not rely upon his friends, and who does not have recourse to a ruler. If what is meant is that the created person upon whom reliance is placed has the ability to regulate and dispose of the affairs of the world, independently of divine command, then indeed this is *kufr*; otherwise, the practice is entirely harmless.

It will be appropriate to cite here what has been narrated here by al-Qutaybi. He relates that he was once sitting next to the tomb of the Messenger of God—peace and blessings be upon him—when a Bedouin came, offered his salutations to the Messenger, and then recited these verses:

> O best and greatest of those ever buried in the earth, who have made it fragrant with their perfume,
> May my soul be a ransom for the tomb in which you dwell , for there lie purity, and generosity, and nobility.

The Bedouin then said: "Here I am, o Messenger of God; I have wronged myself. I seek forgiveness of God and I ask you, o Messenger of God, that you seek forgiveness for me." Al-Qutaybi relates that he then fell asleep, and dreamed that the Prophet told him: "O Qutaybi, find the Bedouin, and give him the glad tidings that God has forgiven him." He accordingly rose and gave the Bedouin the good news.

—(From *Manhaj al-Rashad li man aran al-Sadad*, printed as appendix to Muhammad Husayn Kashif al-Ghita', *al-'Abaqat al-'Anbariya fi 'l-Tabaqat al-Ja'fariya*, ed. Jaudat al-Qazwini, Beirut, 1417/1998, p. 555).

CHRONOLOGY

1115/1703	Birth of Muhammad b. 'Abd al-Wahhab in 'Uyayna
1139/1726	Dismissal of his father from judgeship of 'Uyayna, compelled to move to Huraymila
1140/1727	Muhammad b. 'Abd al-Wahhab embarks on four years of study in Medina
1145/1732	He moves to al-Majmu'a, near Basra
1146/1733	His delegation to Mecca seeking permission to make the *hajj* is defeated in debate with the *'ulama*
1153/1740	His father dies; he returns to al-'Uyayna, concludes a pact with its ruler, 'Uthman b. Mu'ammar
1157/1744	He moves to al-Dir'iya; concludes a pact with Muhammad b. Sa'ud, thus founding the Wahhabi-Saudi alliance
1159/1746	Wahhabi-Saudi state declares *jihad* against Muslims
1180/1766	Death of Muhammad b. 'Abd al-Wahhab
1217/1802	Wahhabi massacre and plundering of Karbala
1217/1803	Wahhabi massacre of Ta'if; first Wahhabi occupation of Mecca
1218/1803	Assassination of 'Abd al-'Aziz b. Muhammad b. Sa'ud
1220/1805	Wahhabi conquest of Medina
1220/1806	Second Wahhabi conquest of Mecca

1228/1813	Liberation of Mecca and Medina by Muhammad 'Ali Pasha
1234/1819	Sacking of al-Dir'iyya by Muhammad 'Ali Pasha; execution of 'Abdullah b. Sa'ud in Istanbul
1865	First British contact with the Saudi family
1915	Anglo-Saudi Treaty
1924–1925	Saudi conquest of the Hijaz
1929	Suppression of the Ikhwan
1932	Formal proclamation of the Kingdom of Saudi Arabia
1953	Death of 'Abd al-'Aziz b. Sa'ud
1962	Foundation of Muslim World League
1979	Uprising in Mecca
1981	Gulf War
1993	Establishment of Committee for Legitimate Rights
2001	End of Taliban regime in Afghanistan

BIBLIOGRAPHY

a) **Writings of Muhammad b. 'Abd al-Wahhab:**

Kashf al-Shubuhat, expanded and annotated by 'Ali al-Hamad al-Salihi, with a postscript by 'Abd al-Rahman Muhammad al-Dusari, Riyad, 1388/1968.

Kitab al-Tawhid, translated, introduced and expanded by Isma'il al-Faruqi, Delhi, 1988.

Masa'il al-Jahiliyya, expanded by Mahmud Shukri al-Alusi, Mecca, n.d.

Mu'allafat al-Shaykh al-Imam Muhammad b. 'Abd al-Wahhab, eds. 'Abd al-'Aziz al-Rumi, Muhammad Baltaci, and Sayyid Hijab, Riyad, n.d., 4(?) vols.

Sources of Islamic Thought: Three Epistles on Tawhid, translated and edited by Isma'il al-Faruqi, Indianapolis, 1980.

b) **Refutations of Wahhabism:**

Da'ud b. Sulayman al-Baghdadi al-Naqshabandi al-Khalidi, *al-Minhat al-Wahbiya fi Radd al-Wahhabiya*, Istanbul, 1305/1887.

Ja'far Kashif al-Ghita', *Manhaj al-Rashad li man arada 'l-Sadad*, printed as appendix to Muhammad Husayn Kashif al-Ghita', *al-'Abaqat al-'Anbariya fi 'l-Tabaqat al-Ja'fariya*, ed. Jaudat al-Qazwini, Beirut, 1418/1998, pp. 505–587.

Khwaja Muhammad Hasan Jan Sahib Sirhindi Mujaddidi, *al-Usul al-Arba'a fi Tardid al-Wahhabiya*, Peshawar, 1346/1928.

Mufti Mahmud Peshawari, *Radd-i Wahhabi*, Delhi, 1264/1848.

Muhammad Husayn Kashif al-Ghita', *Naqd Fatawa al-Wahhabiya*, Qum, 1416/1995.

Sulayman b. 'Abd al-Wahhab al-Najdi, *al-Sawa'iq al-Ilahiya fi 'l-Radd 'ala 'l-Wahhabiya*, reprint, Istanbul, 1396/1976.

(The foregoing represents only a selection of the more significant and accessible titles; for an exhaustive list of works written in refutation of Wahhabism and the doctrines and persons associated with it, see al-Sayyid 'Abdullah Muhammad

'Ali, "Mu'jam ma allafahu 'ulama' al-ummat al-islamiyya li 'l-radd 'ala khurafat al-da'wat al-wahhabiya," *Turathuna*, no. 18, Shawwal 1409, pp. 866–898).

c) Other sources:

Aburish, Said K. *The rise, corruption, and coming fall of the House of Saud*, London, 1994.

Asad, Muhammad *The Road to Mecca*, London, 1954

Burckhardt, J.L. *Notes on the Bedouins and Wahabys*, London, 1830

Çağatay, Neşet "Vehhabilik," *Islam Ansiklopedisi*, XIII, pp. 262–269.

de Gaury, Gerald *Rulers of Mecca*, London, 1951

Eyüb Sabri Pasha *Tarih-i Vehhabiyan*, Istanbul, 1296/1879.

Fandi, Mamoun *Saudi Arabia and the Politics of Dissent*, New York, 1999

Laoust, Henri "Ibn 'Abd al-Wahhâb, Muhammad," *Encyclopaedia of Islam* (new edition), III, pp. 677–679.

Noelle, Christine "The Anti-Wahhabi Reaction in Nineteenth Century Afghanistan," *Muslim World*, LVIIIV (1995), pp. 23–48.

Peskes, Esther and Werner Ende "Wahhâbiyya," *Encyclopaedia of Islam* (new edition), X, pp. 39–47 (with detailed bibliographies on pp. 45, 46–47).

Rashid, Ahmed *Taliban*, London and New Haven, 2000.

Safiullah, Sheikh M. "Wahhabism: A Conceptual Relationship Between Muhammad Ibn 'Abd al-Wahhab and Taqiyy al-Din Ahmad Ibn Taymiyya," *Hamdard Islamicus*, X/1 (1987), pp. 67–83.

'Uthman b. 'Abdullah b. Bishr *'Unwan al-Majd fi Tarikh Najd*, Riyadh, n.d.

Winder, R. Bayly *Saudi Arabia in the Nineteenth Century*, New York, 1980

INDEX

89

MIZAN PUBLICATIONS
available from
ISLAMIC PUBLICATIONS INTERNATIONAL

On the Sociology of Islam by Ali Shari'ati tr. by Hamid Algar
Paperback ISBN 0-933782-00-4 $ 9.95

Marxism and Other Western Fallacies: An Islamic Critique by Ali Shari'ati
tr. Robert Campbell
Paperback ISBN 0-933782-06-3 $ 9.95 Hardback ISBN 0-933782-05-5 $ 19.95

Constitution of the Islamic Republic of Iran tr. Hamid Algar
Paperback ISBN 0-933782-07-1 $ 4.95 Hardback ISBN 0-933782-02-0 $ 14.95

Islam and Revolution: Writings and Declaration of Imam Khomeini
tr. Hamid Algar
Paperback ISBN 0-933782-03-9 $ 19.95 Hardback ISBN 0-933782-04-7 $ 29.95

The Islamic Struggle in Syria by Umar F. Abd-Allah
Hardback ISBN 0-933782-10-1 $ 29.95

Occidentosis: A Plague from the West by Jalal Al-i Ahmad tr. Robert Campbell
Paperback ISBN 0-933782-13-6 $ 9.95 Hardback ISBN 0-933782-12-8 $ 19.95

The Contemporary Muslim Movement in the Philippines by Cesar Adib Majul
Paperback ISBN 0-933782-17-9 $ 9.95 Hardback ISBN 0-933782-16-9 $ 19.95

Fundamental of Islamic Thought: God, Man and the Universe
by Ayatullah Murtaza Mutahhari tr. Robert Campbell
Paperback ISBN 0-933782-15-2 $ 9.95

Social and Historical Change: An Islamic Perspective
by Ayatullah Murtaza Mutahhari tr. by Robert Campbell
Paperback ISBN 0-933782-19-5 $ 9.95 Hardback ISBN 0-933782-18-7 $ 19.95

Principles of Sufism by Al-Qushayri tr. B. R. Von Schlegell
Paperback ISBN 0-933782-20-9 $ 19.95 Hardback ISBN 0-933782-21-7 $ 29.95

Also available are the following Islamic Book Trust publications:

Modern Islamic Political Thought by Hamid Enyat, Foreword by Hamid Algar
Paperback ISBN 983-9154-15-X $ 24.95

The Qur'anic Phenomenon by Malik Bennabi
tr. by Mohamed el-Tahir el-Mesawi Paperback ISBN 983-9154-25-7 $ 24.95

Ghazali and Prayer by Kojiro Nakamura
Paperback ISBN 983-9154-36-2 $ 24.95

The Quranic Foundations and Structure of Muslim Society
by Dr. Fazl-ur-Rahman Ansari
Paperback (2 Volumes) ISBN 1-889999-32-6 $ 79.95

Also published by
ISLAMIC PUBLICATIONS
INTERNATIONAL

Surat Al-Fatiha: Foundation of the Qur'an by Hamid Algar
Paperback ISBN 1-889999-00-8 $ 5.95

Sufism: Principles and Practice by Hamid Algar
Paperback ISBN 1-889999-02-4 $ 5.95

Jesus In The Qur'an: His Reality Expounded in the Qur'an
by Hamid Algar
Paperback ISBN 1-889999-09-1 $ 5.95

**Understanding The Four Madhhabs: The Facts about
Ijtihad and Taqlid**
by Abdal Hakim Murad (T.J. Winters)
Paperback ISBN 1-889999-07-5 $ 3.00

The Sunnah: Its Obligatory and Exemplary Aspects by Hamid Algar
Paperback ISBN 1-889999-01-6 $ 5.95

Imam Abu Hamid Ghazali: An Exponent of Islam in Its Totality
by Hamid Algar
Paperback ISBN 1-889999-15-6 $ 5.95

Hasan Al-Banna: Founder of the First Modern Islamic Movement
by Hamid Algar
Paperback ISBN # 1-889999-18-0 $ 8.95

**Roots of The Islamic Revolution in Iran/Four Lectures/Revised &
Expanded Edition** by Hamid Algar
Paperback ISBN # 1-889999-26-1 $ 14.95
Hardback ISBN # 1-889999-27-X $ 24.95

Social Justice in Islam by Sayyid Qutb
Translation Revised and Introduction by Hamid Algar
Paperback ISBN # 1-889999-11-3 $ 19.95
Hardback ISBN # 1-889999-12-1 $ 29.95

Sales Tax: Please add 7% for books shipped to New York address.
Shipping: $4.00 for the first book and $ 1.00 for additional publication